Let's call it
FIESTA

Edouard Seidler

Let's call it FIESTA

The Auto-biography of Ford's project Bobcat

HAESSNER PUBLISHING, INC.

WITH

EDITA · LAUSANNE

BY THE SAME AUTHOR

The Romance of Renault (Edita 1973)
World Champion (Edita 1970)
The great voices of the automobile (L'Equipe 1970)
Sports and the Press (A. Colin 1964)
Dictionary of Sports (Seghers 1963)
French Rugby (Gautier 1961)
Labor in Virginia (Institute for Advanced Study, Princeton 1954)

Library of Congress Card No: 77-74639
ISBN 0-87799-015-8

Haessner Publishing, Inc.
Newfoundland, New Jersey 07435

Printed in the United States of America

CONTENTS

*Nothing is understandable except
through its history.*

Father Teilhard de Chardin

*We must throw a bridge between
Europe and the United States of America*

Henry Ford I (1924)

*Extinct by instinct
Paralysis by analysis*

Industrial motto of unknown origin

*The devil learned more from experience
than from being the devil.*

Benito Lorenz

For Hélène who respects,
Rhoda who loves,
Catherine and Marianne who tolerate cars...

Already a true 'European' at an early age, Henry Ford II accompanied his father Edsel Ford (right) to the laying of the cornerstone of the Dagenham plant in England.

INTRODUCTION...

September, 1973, Coronado Beach in Southern California. Henry Ford II was showing his new range of cars to the international press. The star of the show was the Mustang II, a smaller, lighter car to replace the original Mustang. Several European journalists had made the trip. They were thinking small, too. Above all, they wanted to know if Ford would ever build a really small car in Europe, smaller and lighter than the Escort.

Henry Ford said: 'It's a luxury we haven't allowed ourselves up to now. Maybe soon the luxury we shall not be able to afford will be that of not *making such a car.'*

That night in private, he revealed a little more: 'We've done a most serious and detailed study of a small car', he told me. 'We haven't yet taken the final decision to make it, but there's a good chance we shall do so before the end of the year.'

'Where would you build it?'

'In Spain, probably, but perhaps in other places, too. This could be Ford's first world car.'

'Would you also sell it in the United States?'

'Quite likely. And we might make it eventually in Brazil, too, in Australia, even in America. I've always believed in little cars, but we simply didn't know how to make them at a reasonable and competitive price. Thanks to the research that we're now doing we may manage it.'

And so I learned that the 'Bobcat project'—code name given to the new car—could well turn out to be the biggest in the whole history of the automobile. The budget for design, development, and production, together with the investment necessary to make it in Spain, was going to amount to more than a billion dollars.

'It's enormous', said Henry Ford. 'Never before has our Company got itself so deeply involved. I reckon that overall it's the

9

most important project in the history of the automobile, certainly in the western world.'

'When will you decide?'

'Probably in December.'

'It would be interesting to write a book about all this!'

'There's been a stack of books on Detroit and on the automobile industry. I've helped several authors with their research. But I've always been disappointed.'

'Novels?'

'Yes, mostly.'

'What I would like to write is not a novel, but the true story of your new car. Explain your problems, go into the details of your design studies. Look for the men behind the concrete of the factories and the sheet metal of the cars themselves.'

'That could be interesting,' said Walter Hayes, Vice President of Ford Europe in charge of public affairs. 'Especially if the book came out at the same time as the car.'

Henry Ford demurred: 'But it's still a highly secret project.'

'I know how to hold my tongue.'

'Well, what do you want to know? What would you need to write a book like that?'

'I want to know everything, to meet everyone involved in the project. Get them to talk. See their figures. Find out why they made their decisions. Their problems, their targets, and the resources employed to meet them.'

'You want to strip us naked!'

I laughed.

'OK', said Henry Ford. 'If we decide to do the car, you can do your book.'

On 3 December, 1973, Henry Ford and his board of directors made their decision. The energy crisis, which made the addition of a baby car to the range more urgent than ever, had removed the last obstacles to the Bobcat project. The plans call for an immense operation involving all of Western Europe, with provisions for extending it eventually to cover the whole planet. Some 500,000 units of a single model are to be built every year, starting in 1976-1977. Engines will be built in Spain, in an entirely new factory near Valencia. Transaxles will be made in France, at Blanquefort, near Bordeaux, where a second factory is to be built alongside the first one, completed in 1973, which already makes automatic transmissions for the whole Ford group. Other parts will come from Eire, England and Germany. The cars will be assembled in Spain, at Saarlouis in Germany where the factory will be extended for the purpose, and at Dagenham in Britain. All told, Ford will have invested over a billion dollars just to make this one car, the biggest outlay ever made by Ford to build the smallest car they have ever produced.

Long after they had decided to make the car, there were still doubts and hesitations, and some people were still ready to question the validity of the whole project. But the show was on the road. It could no longer be stopped. With it went, perhaps, the whole future of the world's second car manufacturer, the strongest of the American 'greats' in Europe.

Ford-Europe at the end of 1973 was producing 1,400,000 vehicles a year, roughly the same as the French Renault-Saviem group. Only Volkswagen and Fiat were bigger than Ford on the European continent, but Ford was selling nearly as many cars there as the other two did because Ford exported fewer

11

vehicles outside Europe. Local factories in America (United States, Canada and Brazil mainly), in Asia, and Australia look after the needs of these areas. The new car was essential to maintain the group's position in Europe at a time when the Fiat 127, the Renault 5, and the Volkswagen Golf and Polo had come to dominate the market.

This book is the history of this car, right from the time when its construction seemed out of the question up to its launching in Europe and in the United States.

But this is intended to be more than just the technical history of a motor car. Behind the few hundred pounds of steel, iron, sheet metal, rubber and plastics, we have tried to reveal the men, the methods, and the problems involved in its birth, recount the battles that had to be fought, discover the techniques that were employed.

My hope is that these pages will show how man, with all his weaknesses, but also with his imagination, his initiative, his enthusiasm, and his individualism somehow manages to triumph over the constraints and the obligations imposed upon him by one of the most tightly structured organisations in the industrial world.

Many books have been written about the world of the automobile. Quite a few were no more than caricatures. This book is an attempt to present a faithful narrative of a true industrial adventure. It has been possible to write it only because Ford at all levels have played the game, loyally and completely. In Detroit and Merkenich, at Dunton and Saarlouis, at Bordeaux, Valencia and Madrid, I have watched the daily life of the men, the factories and the cars for three years and nothing has been hidden from me. Documents, normally secret, were freely made available. Naturally, I have had to choose between the recollections, sometimes blurred, of the men who were engaged on the project, and check some of their verbal accounts against Ford's archives in order to get at the real truth of this great adventure.

I have been greatly helped by Henry Ford himself who was the first to accept the idea of this book; then by all the staffs of the corporation in the United States and in Europe who were good enough to give me some of their precious time. I would particularly like to express my thanks to Mr Lee Iacocca, President of the Corporation, Bill Bourke, who was Chairman of Ford Europe when Bobcat was being developed and who now heads north American Operations, Hal Sperlich, Vice President of the Corporation, John McDougall, President and then chairman of Ford Europe, Bob Lutz, President of Ford Germany, Carl Levy, President of Ford Spain and to their closest associates. Walter Hayes, Geoffrey Howard, who was Technical Editor of Autocar before joining Ford's public relations team, Bob Tarlton at Dearborn, Robert Sicot in Paris, Abilio Bernaldo de Quiros in Madrid and John Southgate in London have given me invaluable help for which I would like to express my gratitude.

I owe very special thanks to my friend and colleague Gordon Wilkins, who provided his assistance for the translation of this book—originally written in French—into English. He did so not only with talent, but also with passion.

Finally, I would like to pay particular tribute to the 135,000 Ford men and women in Europe whose job it now is to guarantee the production, sale and success of the Ford Fiesta, and to the thousands who will work at promoting it in the U.S.

This is only the history of its birth. One day, perhaps, someone will write its life story.

THIS YOU MUST KNOW...
TO UNDERSTAND WHAT FOLLOWS...

Car manufacturers divide the market into a certain number of classes. In Europe, Ford:

— Does not make Class A vehicles (three-wheelers).
— Does not make cars in Class A/B (like the Fiat 126).
— Used not to make cars in Class B (e.g. Fiat 127, Renault 5, Volkswagen Polo).
— Does make cars in Class C (Escort).
— Does make cars in Class C/D (Taunus, Cortina).
— Does make cars in Class D (Consul/Granada).
— Does not make cars in Class E (e.g. BMW 525, Mercedes-Benz 250/280).
— Does not make cars in Class F (e.g. Rolls-Royce, Lamborghini, etc.).

*

Ford was the first Anglo-Saxon manufacturer to adopt the metric system so as to create a common language between Ford of Britain and Ford Werke in Germany, when Ford of Europe was created in 1967.

*

Ford's accounting unit is the dollar. It has seen a lot of ups and downs in the course of the story which follows. On 1 January 1977, the dollar was worth

2.37 DM at Frankfurt
4.99 FF in Paris
68.97 Pesetas in Madrid
£0.59 in London
2.45 sf in Zurich

BUDGET FOR A TASK FORCE

'I need 200,000 dollars, Ralph. With 200,000 dollars, I can make it.'

'200,000 dollars?'

'We'll get together a small task force. Not more than ten guys. We'll have to do it in Germany. The Germans are great at producing prototypes. Get me 200,000 dollars and in a year you'll have a mock-up, a serious proposition, figures, everything.'

'We'll look into it, Jim. We'll see.'

Ralph Peters had come from Detroit where he was responsible for product planning at Lincoln-Mercury. He was enthusiastic, a ready talker, a charmer, and a spell-binder. Two years earlier, in June, 1967, Henry Ford had decided to give his main European subsidiaries, Ford Werke at Cologne and Ford of Britain in England, a single identity by creating an integrated Continental organisation, Ford of Europe.

'There's only one Volkswagen in Europe, only one Fiat, one Renault,' said Henry Ford. 'Why do we need a mosaic of Fords? We must co-ordinate our efforts and try to integrate our resources.'

The small Escort, first truly 'European' Ford, was then being developed. It was to be produced simultaneously in Britain and Germany, assembled at Halewood and Saarlouis.

In April 1969, Peters was appointed Vice President for Product Planning of Ford of Europe. Some months earlier, Jim Donaldson had become Advanced Planning Manager. He was only 25. Dark, stocky, square-shouldered, he looked as if he might have played scrum half in the Scottish fifteen, or boxed as a bantam. Obviously he carried a punch. Donaldson had spent some time studying political science, economics, and psychology. But most of what he knew, and what he was now discussing in a rich and rocky Scots accent, he had learned at Ford. He had not been surprised when Ralph Peters had called him in to run over the Ford range and raise the question of a possible small car.

'With the Escort', said Peters, 'we are represented in Class C. With Taunus and Cortina we have good C/D cars. We're going to move up a rung in 1972 with the Granada. If Europe reacts like America, we'll have problems with the Capri just as we've had over there with the Mustang. But we have nothing, nothing at all in Class B. Fiat, Renault, British Leyland are in it. Not us. What can we do?'

Donaldson suppressed a smile. The B-car at Ford was like the Loch Ness Monster. Everyone talked about it, but no one ever saw it. For years Henry Ford himself had been raising it. Twice a year, at the top management meetings over which he presided in Europe, the problem of the B-car was on the agenda. Henry Ford is temperamentally in favour of small cars. Several times in the past he had approved projects for design studies aimed at the evolution of a small-size low-cost vehicle. The appearance in England of the 'Mini' which Alec Issigonis and BMC launched in 1959 sparked off a whole series of Ford projects which came to nothing. At the beginning of the sixties Terry Beckett, the Cortina man, who was later to become chairman of Ford of Britain, had built at the centre for Advanced Studies in Birmingham a prototype which, like the others, was soon consigned to limbo.

It had been the same story for years. Product men in London and Cologne had just one idea in mind; to convince the hierarchy to launch a small European car, much smaller than the German Taunus, smaller than the British Anglia, smaller even than the future Escort. They had their eyes on Fiat, Renault, and BMC, who were moving ahead, thanks to the models they had at the bottom end of the range. They examined the Latin markets, France and Italy, which were dominated by several 'non-cars' such as the Renault 4, Citroen 2 CV, Fiat 500 and Fiat 600, but also a whole series of cars and engines under one litre capacity which had been or were being

18

brought into existence by fiscal regulations favouring economical cars with tiny engines.

For them, Ford suffered quite a handicap in these markets. Only a small Ford could put Ford in the running. But the conclusion was always the same; to build such a car, competitive in quality, is not possible if one must maintain certain indispensable criteria on profitability.

Whenever a new product planning chief arrived, he knew straight away what they would expect him to do: renovate the existing models. He was also well briefed on what he could not do. In Europe, as everyone knows, Ford does not produce convertibles, taxis, true sports cars, or super luxury cars.

'But we're the champions in popular cars' he said to himself. 'Value for money. The maximum of amenities at the keenest possible price. That's our credo. So why not a mini?'

For the men whose job it is to define future products in technical terms, the temptation is natural, even obvious. The religion of the Company lies in the successful product. The great apostles grouped round Ford are all men who at some time have staked their destinies on a revolutionary model. Lee Iacocca is 'Mr Mustang'. The success of the Mustang was to propel him to the Presidency of Ford. Terry Beckett is 'Mr Cortina' and was to become chairman of Ford of Britain. So who was to become 'Mr B-car', the man of the mini?

'Let's make a small car', said Peters to Donaldson.

'O.K. Ralph. We can try. But don't let's do it just on paper. If we want to convince them, we've got to show them something real. Something that looks like a car'.

For here, once again, history goes on repeating itself, and Donaldson was paid to know just that. Every time the Finance men heard talk of small cars they puckered their eyebrows.

'Mini cars, mini profits,' they said.

It had become a refrain which ended dozens of projects. Others before Peters and Donaldson had bitten the dust. They had taken what was available, an Anglia, a Taunus. They had cut down the bodywork, thus saving a few inches of sheet metal in front, chopped the boot at the rear, and reduced the cylinder capacity of the engine.

Verdict of the Engineers:

'Sure, it's small. But it's bad.'

Verdict of the Financiers:

'Yes, it's small, but it will cost almost as much as if it were larger. The length of a car doesn't matter to the factories, to the tooling or to the men on the line. Three metres, four metres, five metres, it's still a car, gentlemen. Agreed, you save a little sheet metal here and there, but you still need the same number of men and machine tools to make it.'

Verdict of the Marketing Men:

'There's no hurry. Europe won't always be buying small cars. It's going to get richer. That will be the end of the Class B cars. Very soon the market will begin with the C class cars.'

It was a tale that was repeated regularly. There were those who wanted to build a small car and those who considered such a project useless or too costly and, in any case, impossible. Then someone would say: 'Besides, Fiat and Renault don't make anything out of their small cars'. And they passed on to the next item on the agenda.

*

However, something happened at the end of the sixties. Suddenly, the United States discovered that perhaps the Americans themselves were ready to drive short, cropped, compact cars; functional vehicles rather than motorised drawing-rooms. Volkswagen continued to unload thousands of cars at American ports and the Japanese in their turn emerged victorious from their first assault on the world's greatest car market. Those who had forever been predicting the death of the Beetle began to ask themselves if perhaps they had been wrong. And in the secret experimental departments in Detroit, engineers and stylists evolved the cars that would have been dismissed as impossible only a few years earlier: a Gremlin at American Motors, a Pinto at Ford, a Vega at General Motors; American cars scaled down and sometimes powered by small European four-cylinder engines.

20

They worked on cars like these because it had become an absolute necessity. Just think: Chrysler was no longer number three on the market. Number three was the importers! Something had to be found to seal off the breach and prevent their establishing a permanent hold on more than 20 per cent of the market.

Nevertheless, necessity was not the only motivation. They were also taking a gamble which was by no means stupid. A small car, they wagered, need not necessarily be stripped-down and cheap. Just because it is compact and has a small engine, a car need not lack comfort or charm, need not be deprived of optional equipment delivered at extra cost. The gamble embarked upon by those who conceived the Pinto was that they could sell 400,000 units a year, and that these would be equipped with automatic transmissions, with stereo sound and—why not?—even air-conditioning. There would be versions with thick carpeting, velvet upholstery, bucket seats, a whole range of optional equipment which in short would not mean that they were risking bankruptcy by launching the smallest and most economical American cars ever to emerge from Detroit since the black Model T Ford.

'We stand a chance now,' said Donaldson to Peters. 'The climate is changing. With 200,000 dollars, 10 men and a year ahead of us, I can give you something that will convince them.'

*

It was not yet six months since Donaldson had become responsible for advanced studies, that is, for defining pre-prototype concepts which would give birth to new models five to seven years later. However, he already knew that to succeed in a completely new field and then to sell his project to the hierarchy he would have to begin by producing at least a full-sized mock up. When you swim against the current, simple reports, however well documented, are not enough. You must have something tangible to show, something capable of inspiring and firing up their imagination. Besides a detailed report with figures, there had to be, if not a prototype in working order, at least a full scale mock-up of the proposed car and a mock-up of the interior to provide seats for the people who were to pass judgment on the project.

Now Donaldson understood also that such a project would be difficult to bring to fruition with the usual personnel in the usual workshops and studios. He must have a separate budget and get permission to mobilise a small specialised task force, a real commando, which would operate with complete independence outside the conventional channels.

And finally, he knew that he had a fight on his hands.

*

As a multi-national company established on the five continents, employing a total of 450,000 people, Ford necessarily has rigid structures. Tasks, functions, and responsibilities are clearly defined. Precise systems of communication from bottom to top and from top to bottom guarantee at the same time the widest possible information and participation, the possibilities of expression at all levels, and the exercise of individual initiative within the limits imposed by accepted discipline.

There are committees at all levels where information can be passed on and ideas worked out. Yet it is as far removed as possible from anything like military system. Obviously, the final decision can be taken only by top management, but countless other ranks are involved in the preliminary skirmishes which lead up to the final decision. And no one usually pulls rank at those stages. A committee is a battlefield where everyone brings up his own armament, free to give expression to what he believes to be the truth, free to fight for victory, courteously but firmly, without worrying about the rank of those around him.

It is a question of selling; selling one's ideas, studies, and projects, of knowing how to demonstrate, to beguile, to attract, to prove, to convince.

It is as if every executive, trying to get a project accepted, fix a target, or demonstrate a proposal, found himself confronted by ten others demanding:

'Why?'

'Prove it!'

'How will it work?'

'What's in it for us?'

Everything, or almost everything, is called into question, weighed up, dissected, challenged; it is scepticism elevated into a system, a Cartesian philosophy anglo-saxon style, which keeps the men and the company in perpetual motion, in a constant ferment.

Yet there is nothing negative in such a method, in so far as its sole object is to stimulate proof, to restrain some incorrigible enthusiasts, and to distinguish the certainties from the areas of doubt, the opportunities from the risks.

When, finally, the idea, the project, or the target is accepted, it becomes law for everyone from then on and everyone lives for it. That is, until an executive more imaginative or more dynamic than the others perhaps, or new circumstances, or an opportunity hitherto unnoticed, calls everything into question once more.

So the whole process begins all over again: attack-defence, evidence for and against, accelerator and brake. Targets are fixed only to be exceeded, deadlines only to be brought forward. When the apparatus is first set in motion, it is heavy, tenacious, and obstinate, like a carthorse. But when necessary, it can produce the reactions of a thoroughbred. The Mustang horse is not merely one of Ford's greatest successes. It is also a symbol in a company where the rodeo never stops.

The challenge is perpetual, the race goes on for ever, the rider must always expect to see new obstacles raised up before him. When they try to unseat him it is not for fun; it is part of the system. Everyone with a case to argue finds others opposite him who set themselves up as the devil's advocates, determined to deny him a clear run.

Yet they are not really opponents, these men who perseveringly erect the barricades that the others must surmount. On the contrary they are team mates, and they are put there only to check out one of their own colleague's ideas.

When he has victoriously overcome all the obstacles they have put in his way, they all run forward together, in the same direction and towards the same goal. The idea which has broken down the barricades has in effect become everyone's idea. It no longer has any identity save that of the group. From then on they will all fight together to bring it to a successful conclusion.

*

On 30 September 1969, Ralph Peters and Jim Donaldson went into battle. The Product Committee before which they had to defend their project comprised the top brass of Ford of Europe: chairman, president, vice presidents of engineering, design, finance, manufacturing, marketing, and sales.

The objective of Peters and Donaldson was to get the green light for the creation of a task force authorised to do a design study for a Class B car and to get the necessary financial backing. Before the meeting, Peters had provided members of the Committee with a detailed report on his objectives. Now he developed his arguments: 'It is obvious that in a long term view,' he said, 'our company can no longer afford to ignore the Class B cars.'

'Why not?' retorted the finance man. 'We've been ignoring them for ten years and we haven't done so badly at that.'

'We thought that the B's would disappear. On the contrary, they're still there', said Peters. '20 per cent of the whole European market; much more in Italy and France. Fiat and Renault are going to bring out new ones, according to our information. We can't continue to stay out.'

'We've talked this over twenty times and we know for sure that we're not going to do much better than the Escort in total weight and in production cost.'

'In fact,' said Peters 'we don't know any such thing. All the studies that we have done up to now were built on faulty foundations. We started off with known data and existing

24

mechanical parts, and we asked ourselves: "What can we do with all this to make something smaller, lighter, and cheaper?" The results of these studies, I freely admit, have always been disappointing. What we want to do is to start again from scratch, take a close look at all the competitors' cars, establish what is the ideal car for this class, and decide whether we might do better with entirely new mechanical parts.'

'No doubt you are going to suggest front wheel drive?'

'Not necessarily. We want to start with no preconceived ideas', replied Donaldson, 'God knows, we might have to buy mechanical parts from the Japanese or the Patagonians to get our costs down. We might come to the conclusion that we'd have to make the car in one of the countries of the Third World. I don't know. All we want is to tackle the whole problem again with a new approach.'

'We have to look at the way the market is developing', added Peters. 'There are more and more two-car families. We can offer them the large car but not the small one. Perhaps we'd do better to accept a marginal profit on the small car to make sure that Ford has something to offer to the guy who's buying his first vehicle. A little car will add strengh to our dealer network. It might allow us to expand in markets where we are weak or not represented at all. This is what we want to investigate. We want to forget all the previous conclusions and start again with a clean sheet.'

'That's reasonable,' said the chairman. 'How would you do it?'

'We want to form a very small task force, independent of everyone else, with no commitments except to this project. We need a workshop, preferably in Germany. The team would be responsible to Advanced Product Planning. Donaldson would lead it. He will need two research engineers, two production engineers, a cost analyst and four or five assistants'

'No designer?' asked Joe Oros, vice president in charge of design.

'No. No designer', replied Donaldson. 'What we are studying is a concept, not a finished vehicle, all painted and polished. The style doesn't matter.'

'How much do you need?' asked the chairman.

'Two hundred thousand dollars and twelve months,' answered Peters. Those sitting round the table looked at each other. The silence was heavy but brief.

'Good,' said the chairman. 'You can have eight months and one hundred thousand dollars. You start tomorrow. I want a complete report on the state of the job in February, before Mr Ford's visit. Another report in April, which will be studied by this committee. And you will present your final report with all your conclusions next June. O.K.?'

'O.K.,' said Peters.

'O.K.,' echoed Donaldson.

The meeting was ended. In the entrance hall Peters turned to Donaldson.

'It's up to you, my boy. You won't be rich and it won't be easy. But this could be the start of something important. If you succeed, you can always say that you ran the cheapest research programme ever undertaken for a new model.'

'We'll manage,' replied Donaldson in his broad Scots accent. 'We'll manage. We've won the first round. Now we must see it through to the finish.'

'LET'S CALL IT TORINO!'

The team was soon got together. Ford Werke at Cologne provided most of the personnel. At Dunton, Donaldson persuaded George Halford to join the command. Halford was an absolutely first class engine man. He was recovering from a heart attack but was not yet ready to start working full time.

'Alright, Jim,' he said, 'I'll give you a hand, but only four or five hours a day. Gently, gently. Give me a chance!'

From then on Donaldson took to boarding aeroplanes as other people take buses. He lived in London but he spent three days a week at Cologne with his men over there. It was an enthusiastic team. For them Ford-Europe had suddenly become an exciting reality.

They were no longer working just for Britain or for Germany but for Europe, and perhaps for the world. In fact it had been agreed that the work of the group would be used to kill two birds with one stone: while they were busy establishing the outline for a European small car and looking at the possibility of producing it, they were also to think about a 'universal' car which could be sold and perhaps produced in the countries of the Third World.

The latter would be an unsophisticated vehicle, rustic but robust, put together by very simple methods, economical to buy and to use, and easy to maintain. To these general objectives were joined more detailed requirements. It must carry four adults, have a good-sized luggage boot, a maximum speed of 55-60 mph, and acceleration from rest to 50 mph in 25 to 30 seconds. They were to assume a production of 250,000 units a year, which would be additional to the whole of current production by Ford-Europe. As for the price, it was not to be more than 50 to 60 per cent of that of a basic Ford Escort.

However, priority was soon given to the B-car project. In conjunction with the marketing people a plan was drawn up providing for an annual production of 300,000 units, 80 per cent of which would be conquest sales to be added progressively to current production starting in 1976.

Whereas Ford had been completely absent from this sector of the market in 1969, the team forecast that Ford's share of the 'mini' market could reach 13.1 per cent by 1980. Thanks to the arrival of the Mini-Ford, the group's overall penetration in European markets would thus rise from 11.5 per cent in 1968 to 16.8 per cent in 1980.

To start with, Donaldson laid down three possibilities which would form the basis of their preliminary work. The first, which they called the B-Car for lack of any other name, would be an entirely new car using very few existing parts and hopefully priced about 15 to 20 per cent below the Escort. That was the first option. The second variant consisted in evolving a car developed from the Escort and using many of the same components, on condition that it could be sold at a price appreciably lower than that of the Escort. Finally, a third working hypothesis consisted of a shortened, stripped Escort, simplified sufficiently to cut the price by about 10 per cent.

The last of these three options was soon abandoned. The Donaldson team had set their sights higher. They were already beginning to think about front wheel drive and independent suspension all round.

Early in January 1970 the specification took shape. The B Car should not weigh more than 1,400 lbs. (630 kg), say about 340 lbs. less than the Escort. After taking apart all the cars of their competitors they decided that the engine should be something like that of the Fiat 850 and that all means of reducing the capacity of the Kent 1100 engine (that of the Anglia and then of the Escort) should be explored. If they could manage to do front wheel drive, the Autobianchi 112 would serve as an example and as a target in the transverse location of the engine, the layout of the transmission, and the front suspension. Rear suspension could be by a rigid axle as on the Honda 360 or independent as on the Fiat 128.

But at the same time they drew up an outline of a conventional car which could use a transmission and rear axle based on those of the Escort, a front suspension also borrowed from the Escort, and a certain number of other parts drawn from Ford's current range.

Donaldson soon concluded that the project must be conventional in order to be acceptable.

'Whenever I talk about front-wheel drive to some of our finance guys, they stick their hands in their pockets as if I was trying to pinch their notecases,' he told his team. 'Let's be realistic, gentlemen. If we want to end up with a feasible, reasonable, economic proposition, we must work with what we've got already. Let's stick to the Kent engine, but modify the block. Let's decide to use the transmissions we have in stock. We've had one go at front-wheel drive in Germany on the Taunus. They won't let us do that again.'

Little by little, the car took shape. At first on paper. A car is created by bringing together hundreds of separate parts. It is a compromise between an infinite number of decisions over details, but the whole thing always revolves around some twenty-five basic technical definitions, which Ford engineers call the hard points. These are the ones which form the subject of all the discussions, first among the Product Committee, then at a top management meeting. They are not adopted until they have been approved by Henry Ford in person. At Cologne, Donaldson's team—which reported progress weekly to Peters—defined those hard points. Then the various ways to achieve them.

The presence within the team of research engineers, manufacturing experts and cost analysts helped them go ahead at a brisk pace. Soon they were starting construction of the prototype itself. Naturally there was not enough money to build a real vehicle with bodywork in steel or fibreglass. They had to be content with a wooden mock-up covered in plasticine sheet backed up by a mock-up of the interior.

'Let's not try to make it look pretty,' he kept telling his men. 'What we have to produce is a general technical concept. The curvature of the windows and the cross section of the doors is not important, nor is the radiator grille. Our mock-up has to be a box, not a show car.'

In October 1970 the command was on time. Ford-Europe's top brass had been kept regularly informed on the progress of the work, but good care had been taken not to let them see the baby before it was born. Finally the family was summoned to the cradle. The Product Committee of Ford-Europe met at Merkenich's Ford Werke design centre. The immense secret exhibition hall, where, on turntables under the blaze of sun-light projectors, prototypes and new cars are traditionally given an advance showing to the great pontiffs of the corpora-tion, had been completely cleared for the presentation of the new baby.

Worried about what he was going to see—the only creation of Ford-Europe in which the designers could have had no hand—Joe Oros moved around making it clear that he had had no part in it. In an adjoining room, Peters delivered a complete report on the car, before leading the group into the hall where Donaldson's B Car awaited them.

'Never,' he said, 'have we carried our analysis so far. We are convinced that the facts we have accumulated will permit us to take it right through to the finish, up to the development of a real prototype. This is merely the result of a pre-programme. If you agree we will present our conclusions to Henry Ford this winter and ask him for authority to proceed.'

'Alright, Ralph!' said the chairman. 'Let's see your surprise packet.'

The door opened and they entered the great hall. Over there, fifty yards away, a little yellow car stood out against the dark hangings on the walls. Donaldson and his men, their hearts beating hard, stood ready by their mock-ups.

At first no one said anything. They moved around the car with an air of serious concentration. Then one of them sat himself down in the interior mock-up, behind the steering wheel. Another sat down in the front passenger seat, and two more behind.

'It's really smaller than the Escort?' asked someone.

'Yes, sir.'

30

'But there's as much space inside. Perhaps more, I'd say.'

'Yes, sir.'

'But it's great, great,' said someone else.

The team hadn't yet scored a knock-out but they had won the second round. The documentation provided by Peters proved that this car would cost less to produce than any existing Ford. Some people felt the mock-up was already good enough to serve as the basis for a future production model. And furthermore, maybe by lengthening the bodywork, a little here in front, a little there at the rear, they could one day turn this B Car into a C Car without too much in the way of extra tooling investments.

'Very interesting, Ralph. Good work. Well done, Jim. We'll show it to Mr Ford,' said the Chairman, by way of conclusion.

*

For a quarter of a century now, Henry Ford has sat in the same seat at every meeting, first place, at the head of the table. Twice a year, traditionally, he presides over a summit meeting of the European branches of his company. Smiling, strong, jovial, he goes round the table before sitting down. To everyone he is 'Mr Ford', just like his grandfather Henry I, the founder of the dynasty and the inventor of democracy on wheels. No one would presume to call him 'Henry' although even the greatest in our world are known by their first names. He, on the other hand, remembers everyone's first name and uses it. Endowed with an astonishing memory, he enquires about the children, is glad to hear that Peter has entered university, that Suzy got married and that the family is moving into a new house.

When he has shaken hands with everyone, Mr Ford goes back to his chair, takes off his jacket, spreads his various files out on the table, places his packet of Benson and Hedges— later to be replaced by small cigarillos—in front of him, makes sure that everyone is present and then:

'Nice to be here, gentlemen. Let's get down to business...'

But this time it was not Henry Ford who held the attention of the men gathered round the table in the first floor conference room of the research and engineering centre at Dunton, that great block of concrete planted in the Essex countryside, 30 miles out of London. They were not conscious of the wind which battered and bent the leafless trees outside on this grey, rainy day of February, 1971. The man they were looking at was seated on the right of Mr Ford. He calmly returned their gaze. He was solid, square-cut, in his mid-forties with an energetic air. The man was Lee Iacocca. For everyone he was a kind of hero, the incarnation of success the Ford way. Over in America, school children are being taught that any one of them can, given enough talent, ability, good luck, and hard work, become President of the United States. The man now facing them, was for his part the living proof that anyone given the same qualities can become president of Ford.

Lee Iacocca was the man of the Mustang and he was soon to become the father of the Pinto. Some weeks earlier, Henry Ford had made him his right hand man. The previous year, he had taken his first official trip to Europe, which was also a pilgrimage to the source of his family. Son of Italian immigrants—his real first name is Lido, in memory of that holiday resort in the Venetian lagoon where his parents conceived him—he had become a symbol of success, American style. With two engineering diplomas in his pocket, he began his career at Ford at the age of 22. He started in sales and then moved to marketing; he was barely 36 in 1960 when he was made general manager of Ford Division and a corporate vice president. Seven years later, he had become responsible for all Ford activities in North America.

He had been a member of the board since 1965 but this trip was his first as president, as the man with the prime operational responsibility not only in the United States, but also in Europe and the whole world.

Some of those round the table—the top management of Ford in Europe—had already worked with Iacocca. The others knew him only by repute. In no time at all they were going to learn that this reputation was well earned.

'The first item on our agenda today,' said Iacocca, 'is the problem of the B Car.'

The division of responsibilities and functions between Henry Ford, chairman of the company, and Lee Iacocca as president leaves no room for argument. The former is concerned with general policy, overall control and major decisions. He is in a continuing sense the representative of the shareholders and he is the emanation of the board of directors at the heart of the corporation. Nothing essential is ever done in the whole corporation unless it has been approved by Mr Ford.

Iacocca, for his part, has an essentially operational role. It is his job to play a daily and detailed part in the running of the company. He must maintain contact, often on a direct and personal level, with those responsible for the products and their distribution. The president looks at things more closely; the chairman views them in broad principle, at a higher level. In practice, however, it is as simple as can be: Henry Ford is the boss and Lee Iacocca is his right hand man. Over in Detroit their offices are only a few steps from each other on the top floor of that cube of glass, steel and concrete, built on a piece of Dearborn former waste land, which now houses the corporation's world headquarters. Only a length of deep pile carpet separates Henry Ford—first office on the left on leaving the elevator which connects with the executive garage— and Lee Iacocca, further left, at the end of the corridor.

Out here on location, it is Iacocca who conducts the discussions, going straight to the point in his direct and pungent style. His latin temperament comes over, dynamic, often exuberant, his language colourful and cogent. A single word on a plaque prominently placed on a desk in his office sums up the man: 'WIN!' Iacocca is a fighter, a man in a hurry. He puts his shoulder to any obstacle, lets nothing stand in his way. Between himself and his objective, the road he prefers is the shortest and most direct. But in a quarter of a century of pushing ahead at Ford he has learned that a strategic sidestep can sometimes demolish the most formidable obstacles more easily than a direct attack.

He is one of the few who call the boss 'Henry', but then only in private. Here, in front of others, he too addresses him as Mr Ford. He leads the meeting, but he knows very well, as everyone else does, that having listened carefully to everything while smoking his Bensons and sipping his tea, Henry Ford will wind up by asking a few fundamental questions, full of common sense, which no one had thought of before and which quite often can put the whole business back in the melting pot.

*

Donaldson's mock-ups had been installed in an adjoining room, having been brought secretly from Merkenich to Dunton. At the last minute the pre-prototype had been named.

'Let's call it Torino,' suggested Donaldson 'That should please Iacocca.'

In fact, Peters and Donaldson were worried. They felt that their report was sound and that the project would stand up. But they were very conscious of the fact that their mock-up lacked style.

'I think they'll be interested in it, but they're not going to find it very exciting.'

'I've got an idea,' said Peters.

Night was already falling at Dunton, where Ford and Iacocca were expected next day.

'Let's go and see if any of the designers are still around.'

Two or three of them were still there, tidying up their papers and putting away their pencils. Among them was Trevor Erskine, a young and talented lad who was not short of imagination.

'Trevor,' they said, 'will you do something for us ? Just a few sketches. Something that will get one or two guys' mouths watering.'

'O.K.,' said Erskine, 'what is it ?'

They took him out and showed him their mock-up.

'This is the job. We need two or three sexy sketches, if you see what I mean. Forget about the proportions. You can add six inches on the front and maybe four on the back to give it a bit more of a line. Two doors and a fastback. Something a bit Italian, you know? But keep to the height of the roof at the back. We need a real four-seater.'

'O.K.,' said Erskine.

34

Jim Donaldson: 200,000 dollars for a mock-up.

'And not a word to anyone,' warned Peters.

'Alright,' said Erskine, who was tactful enough not to ask any more questions.

Peters and Donaldson knew the risks they were taking. Some things are just not done at Ford. Bypassing regular channels and asking a stylist to do a design without going through the man in charge of the Design department is one of them. Handing out sketches to top management when all one has been asked to do is a technical study with all the figures, that isn't done either.

But it is precisely because there are, here and there, a few independent characters ready to break all the rules, written or traditional, that the Ford Motor Company is an outfit a little different from some other giant corporations, a company with a human face, an enterprise where nothing is impossible and where men like Iacocca can become presidents.

Erskine started work at eight o'clock in the evening. Next morning he arrived with his sketches: three drawings in charcoal which Donaldson immediately had copied. While technically faithful to the mock-up, they were quite attractive.

'Not bad, the Torino!' said Peters.

First drawing, 'something a bit Italian...'

Donaldson had the originals framed to hang in his office. The copies were destined to go much further.

*

Ford, Iacocca and the vice-presidents who had accompanied them from Detroit inspected the Torino. Their verdict was favourable. Henry Ford has always liked small cars. Often, in the summer, during the holidays that he likes to spend on the Côte d'Azur, he arranges to hire one of the small European models which he enjoys driving, and leaves the Fords provided for him in the garage. As for Iacocca, he lights up whenever a new model or an unusual prototype is shown to him. He is fundamentally a product man.

During the six years he had been sitting on the Ford board, he had been hearing lots of talk of the B Car and the impossibility of succeeding in this sector of the market. Now that Europe, like the rest of the world, had come under his jurisdiction, he was determined to move beyond these periodical discussions and do everything necessary to establish Ford in the small car market.

For the moment, he was simply asking questions and listening to the explanations provided by Peters. What he heard pleased him. But he knew that the analysis needed to be carried still further and he already had his own ideas.

On this day however, the last word came from Phil Caldwell, president of Ford Europe who was later to become Iacocca's right hand man for international operations. Caldwell was quite ready to believe that the pre-prototype resulting from the exploratory studies by Peters and Donaldson could evolve into a good car, competitive and commercially viable.

'Like everyone else,' he said, 'I like your mock-up. Your analysis is one of the most serious we have ever done up to now. But there's a problem. Just suppose, Ralph, that we made 300,000 of your cars a year.'

'Yes, Phil.'

'How many out of this total would go to buyers that we wouldn't have had otherwise? How many would represent conquest sales and extra production?'

'Er... 150,000, perhaps 200,000.'

'Right, Ralph, there's the problem. Where would you make them? We just don't have the capacity in our existing plants to produce an extra 200,000 cars.'

And so ended the third round. Everyone thought that the Torino looked like a fine fighter, a sound and valid hope for the future. Perhaps the future would bring the opportunities for it. For the moment at least it had suffered a knock out.

In the hallway, Peters went up to Iacocca.

'Take these,' he said.

He offered him the three Torino sketches. Iacocca looked at them for a moment, then put them in his brief case.

'Thanks, Ralph,' he said. 'I'll take them with me. You've done a good job and we'll be talking about it again, believe me. You haven't wasted your time, or ours.'

HALF OF EUROPE

Once a year, a top level conference devoted to long term forecasts deals with future sales and production volumes. The computers spew forth their predictions as though they were certainties. The marketing men put down their forecasts in black and white, draw their graphs and establish their assumptions: overall analysis of market evolution, development by vehicle categories, figures for estimated penetration by the principal competitors and the relative position of Ford.

By a leakage from a supplier, or more often a revelation in the press, the main projects of all competitors are known.

Out of this jumble of information supplied by economists, salesmen, financiers, and sociologists, top management has to draw concrete, practical, and coherent conclusions to cover a period of five years. And then go into action.

This time, at the beginning of 1971, a certain number of facts permitted no argument. First, the American market had ceased to be the dominating factor on the world automobile map. In 1950, 7,800,000 cars were built in the world. Of this total, 85 per cent had rolled off the assembly lines in North America. Twenty years later, while world-wide production had reached 21,700,000 units, North America's share of this production was only 41 per cent and that of the rest of the world 59 per cent. First conclusion therefore: the car market had become a universal one.

The second lesson that Ford management drew from the worldwide curves resulted from the first. Whereas in 1950 the Ford Motor Company produced 22.4 per cent of all the cars made in the world, its share had dropped to 16.9 per cent twenty years later. Failing a vigorous reaction, Ford's share of world car production would be no more than 15.1 per cent in 1976 and 13.9 per cent in 1980.

'Whether we like it or not, gentlemen, we can't go on for much longer without building a small car', said Henry Ford.

A thought which Lee Iacocca rammed home in his own direct and colourful style.

'We're carrying on like a shoe shop which offers its customers nothing smaller than a size seven on the grounds that the smaller sizes only interest one customer in five, and that they prefer to save money and shelf space by not stocking these sizes. I don't know what you'd think of a shop like that. But if they can't provide shoes for my kids because they only need size four or five, do you think we'll go back to them when they need eights or nines?'

One of the documents which was to be studied by the members of the Volume Committee on this particular day included a list of the small cars which were being prepared by Ford's competitors throughout the world. They knew that in a few weeks Fiat was going to launch the 127. In 1972 they were expecting the Honda Civic, Renault 5 and Fiat 126. Later, according to information gathered by the Competitive Liaison and Car Strategy Planning office, a new Kadett would appear at Opel, a new 1100/1300 series at British Leyland and a C Car from Volkswagen, to be followed by a Volkswagen B Car, a new British Mini and perhaps a Renault 2 in 1975.

'They always tell us the same thing,' went on Iacocca. 'If we get involved in the small car race we are going to lose our shirts. What we should be asking ourselves is this: won't we lose even more if we refuse to move down below the Escort?'

The map of Europe was easy to read as far as Ford was concerned. Ford was second only to Fiat in terms of overall sales on the old continent, but was far from occupying such an enviable position everywhere. Since the French factories at Poissy had been sold to Simca, in 1954, Ford's operational bases had been essentially Germany (where the first Fords had come off the lines in Berlin in 1925 and those in Cologne in 1931), and in Great Britain (where the first Model T tourers were assembled at Manchester in 1911 and the first European Fords built at Dagenham in 1931). Ford essentially remained a North European car maker. In 1970 their market penetration was 26.6 per cent in the United Kingdom, 14.7 per cent in West Germany, 13.3 per cent in Belgium and 12 per cent in the Netherlands. But Ford's share in France and Italy, the prime markets for small cars, rarely rose above 5 per cent. As for Spain, a market closed to imported cars, Fords were practically unknown and unrecognised. In 1970 the company registered there a record total of 562 sales representing barely 0.2 per cent of the market.

'I really think', burst out Iacocca,' that we ought to change our name! We are not Ford-Europe. We are Ford of a half of Europe! And that is what we'll remain as long as we can't provide the cars that the other half wants.'

He went on: 'We can't go on forever importing foreign workers into northern Europe. It's time to go and build our cars in the places where the manpower already exists. Let's export the factories and stop importing the men!'

*

For a long time Henry Ford, a Latin at heart, had been dreaming of a break-out in the direction of Spain. As far back as 1969 he had initiated studies on a possible take-over of Authi, the Spanish assembly concern which was later absorbed by British Leyland, and later still by SEAT. John Andrews, who initiated the integration of Ford-Europe in 1967 ('There is a Common Market, we should have a common company') had never ceased looking southwards; and now there was Lee Iacocca, with Latin blood in his veins, lining up with Henry Ford to establish a new priority, that of southern Europe.

'Let's forget for the moment what we could and should produce in southern Europe,' said Henry Ford, ' let us simply say that come what may, it is down there that we must do something eventually.'

Henry Ford had already promised Georges Pompidou, the Prime Minister and future President of the French Republic that the group's next factory would be built in France if at all possible. And it was in fact at Blanquefort, among the Bordeaux vineyards, that a factory was being built to make automatic transmissions for Ford-Europe.

However, if one was talking about cars, one had to start thinking about Spain. Though a negligible factor ten years earlier, the Spanish market already appeared as one of the principal areas of expansion in Europe. The pace of economic development in Spain had been so swift that the forecasters spoke of a million-car market by 1980.

Yet since the end of the war, Ford had maintained no more than a symbolic presence in Spain. The first cars from the company—five Model A's—had been sold in Spain in 1907. In 1919, Ford had rented a former brewery at Cadiz as an assembly plant for cars and trucks. In 1922 1,132 cars were assembled there. The following year Ford of Spain was transfered to Barcelona. Production increased steadily and in 1930 5,639 cars plus 5,437 trucks left the Spanish assembly lines. Three years later, one car in every three sold in Spain was a Ford.

Nevertheless, customs restrictions and the war were to slow down this expansion and finally stop it. Ford Iberica disappeared completely in 1954, being transformed into Motor Iberica S.A., a company which was no longer controlled by Ford, but merely distributed its products and received some technical assistance. Robert Stevenson, then Ford's vice president in charge of international operations had made a first trip to Madrid in 1970. There he met the Minister for Industry, Lopez de Letona and the Minister of Economic Planning, Lopez Rodo.

'We would like to set up business in Spain,' Stevenson told them.

'Then make us a firm proposition,' replied the Spanish government officials.

*

The forecasts for future production volume showed that in 1976 Ford would need an additional capacity of 140,000 cars simply to handle the demand for the existing range. This was not enough to justify the building of a new factory. In Ford's terms, a factory represents 250,000 units a year.

A report had been produced showing that it would be possible to meet the demand by expanding the existing factories; a little at Dagenham and Halewood in England, a little at Genk in Belgium, a little at Cologne, and rather more at Saarlouis in Germany.

Then Henry Ford said, 'Just suppose we could get a footing in the Spanish market and that we could sell around 100,000 cars there.'

'140,000 and 100,000—that means a new factory,' said Iacocca. 'A Spanish factory!'

*

At Ford of Europe one man had the job of exploring new markets, keeping in touch with the countries where Ford might want to start up a business or expand their activities. Dick Holmes, in charge of New Business Opportunities, was in fact the corporation's top travelling salesman: in Africa one day, in Asia the next, and rarely in his office in London. In order that Ford could have cars smaller than the Escort, he had already tried to negotiate the purchase of DAF, the small Dutch manufacturer in 1969 and again in 1971. These negotiations had come to nothing, and DAF would eventually be absorbed by Sweden's Volvo.

Iacocca now spoke to Holmes.

'Listen, Dick. Get down to Spain and forget everything else. We now have two top priorities: Brazil and Spain. Spain is your job. You must do everything possible to get Ford into Spain. It's vital.'

'What will we make there?'

'I don't know. Taunus, Escort, time will tell. The main thing is to get started. If you succeed, I'll promise you one thing, Dick: we'll put our executive building next to the most beautiful beach on the Spanish coast, we'll give you the best office on the top floor with a view of the sea, and we'll call it the Dick Holmes building!'

SPECIAL ASSISTANT...

Everyone was now agreed that Ford should get established in Spain as quickly as possible. Negotiations were started. In December 1971, Henry Ford entertained Spanish Minister for Industry Lopez de Letona in Detroit and three months later made a return visit to Madrid.

But as for the creation of a new European and perhaps even universal small car, the story went quite differently. Certainly the exploratory efforts by Peters and Donaldson had been well received in Detroit as they had in London and Cologne, but it all came back to the same point in the end. Some felt that to get involved in such a project would be pure folly, guaranteed to break the company. Others claimed that the company would go broke if it did not do it. But still no final and definite conclusions had been drawn about the possibility of making a small car for Europe and the world at a reasonable level of quality, competitiveness, and profitability. No conclusions, that is, apart from the preliminary report by Ralph Peters and the three sketches hurriedly done by Erskine which lay prominently on Lee Iacocca's desk.

In between two committee meetings or two telephone calls, Iacocca would turn back to these sketches and start thinking. If Renault, Fiat, Volkswagen and British Leyland were building or preparing to build mini cars, there could be no real reason why Ford should be incapable of doing likewise. Iacocca just could not believe what had been repeated to him, parrot fashion, for years: 'They don't make any profit on these small cars. In any case, Renault is subsidised by the government ... Fiat receives indirect aid ... this one has the benefit of special wage rates ... and that one is going broke.'

Iacocca had been impressed by the approach chosen in Europe: using a small task force to bypass normal channels and procedures with the job of studying the mini-car question outside the regular routine of the experimental departments and design offices. Without any doubt this was the fastest and most efficient way to do it.

Actually, a similar approach had been used already in the United States. A small team under a former Harvard man, Erik Reickert, had been set up in 1970 to come up with a mini car programme—project 'Nevada'—which never made it past the pre-planning stage.

This time, Iacocca could have given Peters the resources he wanted to push ahead with his investigations. But Europe had other problems to solve at that time and both he and Henry Ford were now so absorbed by the question of the minis that they were no longer content to watch from a distance with the help of trips to Europe: twice or three times a year for Henry Ford, once every two months for Iacocca.

Besides, a small Ford could very quickly find a universal demand. There would be a market for such a car in Brazil and perhaps even in the US, still a Beetle's paradise.

Therefore the best solution to start with would be to mobilise all the resources of the corporation in Detroit itself and give it all possible backing, if they were to persuade themselves, first of all, and then the top management and the board of directors, that Ford should and could give its name to a small car at the bottom of the range, the smallest car ever built by the corporation. After all, the Model T had once made the breakthrough which inaugurated motoring for the masses and Ford had always aimed to produce popular cars. In Europe itself it was Ford who in 1935 launched the £100 car at Dagenham, the 'Popular', the cheapest saloon car which had ever been built up to then.

Iacocca felt that the study done in Europe could serve as a starting point but he needed to find a man capable of moving on from there with maximum efficiency; someone who would not be deterred by the usual taboos, and would not take 'No' for an answer. He did not have far to look, for such a man existed, he knew him well and they had already teamed up in the past. In October, 1971, Hal Sperlich came into the picture.

Sperlich was made of the same stuff as Iacocca. Dashing and direct, he lived on his nerves and refuelled with coffee, which like so many of his colleagues he consumed in prodigious quantities, tea apparently being reserved within the company for Henry Ford and his British colleagues. He was driven by enthusiasm and ambition. Born in Detroit, he had never known and never been interested in anything but cars. Well educated, he had an engineering degree from the University of Michigan and a master's degree in business administration.

Quite early, his path had crossed that of Lee Iacocca who recognised in him one of the best specialists in product planning. When Iacocca conceived the Mustang, a rocket which was to carry him to the top of the company, Hal Sperlich was already his right hand man.

'We think the same way. We work the same way,' said Iacocca later. 'A company like ours needs discipline, but it also needs a few freelance dynamiters like us.'

A year earlier, when he had just turned forty, Sperlich had been appointed vice president of the company and managing director of all the heavy truck activities. But trucks were to be only a short interlude for him.

Iacocca called Sperlich:

'I need you for Europe. Something important.'

'Coming.'

Before he was appointed president upon the departure of 'Bunkie' Knudsen—the former General Motors vice president who swept through Ford like a meteor—Iacocca shared operational responsibilities with Bob Stevenson under the overall control of Henry Ford. Stevenson directed the international operations, but Iacocca's promotion coincided with Stevenson's departure. Iacocca now had no one with him on his personal staff on to whom he could unload the supervision of international operations. He needed a confidential man of business, a permanently available itinerant ambassador. Sperlich was to be just that man.

'I'll make you my Special Assistant,' Iacocca told him. 'You are going to travel. You must meet everyone, see everything, study everything and get to know everything. I want you to put Europe under a magnifying glass with just one idea in mind. I want to know how we can make the best possible B Car; one which will be both competitive and profitable. I want a car for Europe, but also for the rest of the world. This machine could be the first universal Ford since the Model T.'

The first mission that Sperlich embarked upon was a documentary sortie. He started with an empty suitcase and returned with it stuffed full of facts, figures, and analyses. He knew nothing about Europe's problems, but he cheerfully decided to turn that to advantage. He pursued his meticulous enquiries from Cologne to Turin, from Paris to Stockholm, from Madrid to London, and from London to Detroit. For seven or eight months he spent one week out of every two in Europe, crossing the Atlantic as others cross the road. He brought to light all the problems, but also all the opportunities, that were there to be seized by Ford.

'You're lucky,' Henry Ford told him, 'You have nothing to forget, because you don't know anything about the problems we've had and the objections we have run up against. Look at everything without any preconceived ideas. Just remember that Iacocca and I want to get something organised. But you'll soon realise that all the financiers in the company and three-quarters of the management are against a small car. They'd like to have one, but they just don't think it's feasible. Now, you prove otherwise!'

On his first trip to London, Sperlich had lunch with Peters and with him went over all the previous studies which had been done in Europe, none of which had come to anything.

'It's quite simple,' Peters explained, 'We usually succeeded in saving just a few bucks compared with the production cost of an Escort, but we finished up with a car that would have to be sold for a lot less. It didn't make sense.'

'There must be a way,' said Sperlich, 'if we started again from scratch.'

Peters had arrived at the wheel of the latest European small car, the Fiat 127, the little front-drive model from Turin which was to be elected Car of the Year at the end of 1971.

'You must try this!' he said.

Sperlich looked it over. Even before taking the wheel he was impressed by the amount of interior space available in such a compact car.

'It's fantastic!' he said.

He drove the 127 and the impression he formed was no less exciting. It was his first encounter with a European front-drive model, and this encounter was decisive. Swiftly he became convinced that there was no future in making a cut-down 'sub-Escort'. The future car must be a small front-wheel drive. The appearance of the Renault 5 in January, 1972, and the Honda Civic in July only made him more certain.

'It's not going to make things any easier,' he told Iacocca. 'We want to make something cheaper than the Escort and now front-wheel drive is beginning to lead us by the nose. It could save us about twenty pounds in weight but the transmission alone will cost us at the very least an extra fifteen dollars!'

Yet it had to be done. Sperlich was quite certain of it by the time he reached the end of a trip to Europe during which he met the most influential journalists and the best informed technicians in each country. Every market study that he read led to the same conclusion. In Turin, Alessandro de Tomaso, head of Ghia and an associate of Ford, was of the same opinion. Even in Detroit, the best specialists on European cars argued in favour of front-wheel drive for the smaller vehicles.

This was particularly true of Alex Trotman, a young Scot who had been the predecessor of Ralph Peters as head of Product planning for Ford-Europe. Trotman, who wanted to make his career in the United States, had resigned from his position at Dunton in 1969 and had got a new job with Ford in Detroit. He now had a responsible position in the marketing staff but he had struck up a friendship with Sperlich at the time when the latter was the man in charge of Planning in the Ford Division.

From time to time the two men met to exchange ideas. Trotman knew better than anyone what attempts had been made to produce a B Car in Europe during the sixties.

'There's only one serious answer,' he said, 'front-wheel drive. But it will be difficult. You will need a new factory to make

Hal Sperlich, Special Assistant.

the front axles. In a nutshell, you start off with an additional handicap of one hundred million dollars.'

*

While Sperlich was commuting between Detroit and Europe, a small study group had started work under the impatient eye of Lee Iacocca. Whereas General Motors renews its inspiration by internal competition and rivalry between its different divisions, Ford sets study groups and 'think tanks' against each other; often quite small units, which favour the hatching of those 'better ideas' promised in the company's advertisements.

While Sperlich was expected in the first place to bring back a harvest of information and if possible some firm conclusions from his European peregrinations, the group which Iacocca formed in March, 1972, under the leadership of Herb Misch—

who was later to become vice president in charge of environmental problems—was given the task of reviewing everything that had been done in Detroit on small cars, making their own proposals and forecasts on the subject.

To strengthen the group on the technical side, a man who knew the subject from all angles was brought back from Europe four months before he was due to return, Fred Piziali. He had just spent four years at Ford of Europe as vice president for engineering. Teaming up with a styling specialist, Don De La Rosa, an Italo-American like himself, and Iacocca, Piziali set out the pros and cons of all the studies which had been done up to that time.

There had already been a long series of styling studies under the code name of Iris—a dozen different versions of a mini-car based on a Ford Escort chassis—but there was also a prototype christened 'Beta' which had been built by Ghia in Turin.

In collaboration with Gene Bordinat's designers the ideal specification for a European-style mini-car was drawn up and work started on some mock-ups. They were to be called the 'Mini-Mites' and were to play a not unimportant role later.

Before taking the final decision to concentrate the B Car advanced studies at Dearborn itself, Henry Ford had suggested to his general staff in Europe that they should take over the project. On 1 June 1972, a new team had taken charge at Warley. Phil Caldwell had succeeded Paul Lorenz, a financier, as head of Ford-Europe and Bill Bourke had become president. Bourke was 45. With his calm, poise, deep voice, and easy manner, he had an engaging personality, and his rise at Ford had been meteoric. After studying engineering and finance, he started at Ford on the commercial side. He had become sales manager of Ford Canada, then president of Ford Australia, and he had finally supervised the whole of Asia-Pacific region. He had never stayed in one job for more than four years.

'What's your ambition? What do you want to do?', Henry Ford asked him in the course of a long tour of inspection in Asia in 1971.

'Run Europe, one day,' said Bourke. 'In about four or five years, when I am ready for it.'

It did not take Henry Ford that long: one year later, he moved Bourke to London. On his arrival from Australia, he, along with Phil Caldwell, discovered a disturbing situation. Plans for renewing the range of cars were vague. There was no project for the renovation of the Escort and although Ford had just launched the Consul-Granada series, the rest of the range was ageing dangerously.

'We are ready to embark on a serious study for a B Car,' Henry Ford told Caldwell and Bourke. 'We have begun work on it at Detroit. Would you like to take it over?'

'It's too early for us,' said Caldwell. 'We have too much to do for the time being. We must put everything here in order first and give top priority to getting a new Escort ready.'

'Alright,' said Ford. 'Do the Escort in Europe. We'll begin work on the other project at Dearborn.'

Henry Ford and Lee Iacocca then went over the facts again with Sperlich. Without prejudging the nature of the new car to be inserted at the bottom of the range, Sperlich put forward some figures and an idea for an approach to the problem.

Ford and Iacocca knew the figures well already, but being reminded of them only reinforced their determination. Class B and Class C cars (Escort and below) represented almost half of all European new car registrations, but Ford were only represented in this vital section of the market by the Escort, with a penetration not exceeding 7 per cent. Without some rapid and energetic action, Ford were condemned to see their share of European markets dwindling in the course of time. Furthermore, only a small car could give Ford any hope of improving their position in the Latin countries, France and Italy, to say nothing of Spain, where because of the barriers erected against imports, only local production would enable Ford to get a foothold.

Henry Ford and Lee Iacocca knew all this very well and they recognised that there was little chance of pushing forward the design of such a car within the established organisation.

Ford can no longer afford to haggle about the cost, argued Sperlich. To him, there is no point in re-starting for the umpteenth time all that Europe has already tried to do too often on a shoe-string. If Ford is going to produce a universal car it must put everything that's needed into it. This can only be done by setting up a powerful and well-structured task force outside the regular organisation.

So what Donaldson had done with six colleagues and a pittance of 100,000 dollars, was now to get under way with a veritable army, backed by resources which, if not exactly limitless, were the greatest ever brought into play for such a project. In the end, when he had done no more than evolve a pre-prototype, Sperlich would have spent several million dollars and the strength of his private army would have risen to 700.

*

This time Henry Ford and Lee Iacocca were determined to see the job through to the finish and decided in effect to restructure their advanced research activities. A new Product Planning and Research group was thus placed under the command of Hal Sperlich. Its objectives were 'to satisfy itself primarily on the strength of the products over the long term and on a worldwide basis; to carry out all relevant research on vehicles and their components in pursuit of this objective.'

In other words, it was felt that, as problems in a multinational company as important as Ford take on worldwide dimensions, it was necessary to centralise all advanced research and long term investigations within one powerful and well organised body capable of coordinating all the resources of the company in the pursuit of long term objectives. Product Planning and Research would be expected to think, to reflect and conduct the investigations which would precede action for the benefit of all the companies in the group. It was also the logical outcome of that discovery that Ford had ceased to be primarily an American manufacturer and must now consolidate their position as a multinational organisation with a world-wide role to play.

'Quite apart from the B Car project', declared Henry Ford, 'We must put our research on a more systematic basis, strengthen it and create a "Ford system" which will be efficient and consistent, applicable to the whole range of problems that crop up in the company throughout the world.'

Thus Hal Sperlich became the man with the entire responsibility for product planning, thanks to a mini car which had not yet taken shape, which everyone hoped for, but most feared would never see the light, so slender were the chances of making it with a sufficient profit margin.

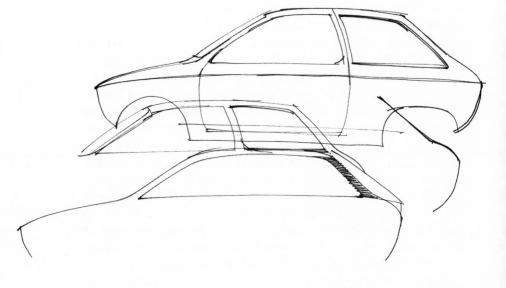

OPERATION BOBCAT

Sperlich built up his team. The advance party which he gathered together was fundamentally European. Only later would he get down to devising a strict plan of organisation for 'PPR'. In the first phase they spoke mainly of a 'New Concepts' office. Responsibility for planning was entrusted to 35-year-old Alex Trotman who had little thought when he abandoned Dunton for Detroit and said goodbye to his native Scotland, that three years later he would again be tackling the problem of a small car for Europe.

The main technical responsibility devolved naturally upon Fred Piziali, who was more committed than ever to the cause of small cars, European style. Jack Collins, who was responsible for engines, had learned his trade with Ford in Latin America. Ron Davies, a Canadian from Australia, was to look after the body. Styling was naturally the job of Don della Rosa and through him, of various competing teams: that of Alessandro de Tomaso and Tom Tjaarda in Turin, that of Uwe Bahnsen at Cologne. Erik Reickert—the man of 1970's project Nevada—and Bob Torkelson, who were later to play a decisive part in the development of the final prototype in Europe and of its launching, were also involved in this original team.

Sperlich only brought in the former Product Planning staff little by little. He himself kept the office in the Design Centre near to Gene Bordinat and his body designers, which he had occupied since the start of his European mission. He installed his team wherever he could find space; some kept their existing offices or moved as squatters into areas that happened to be empty, waiting until they could storm Parklane, a new building which was nearing completion only a few steps from World Headquarters in the middle of the old Dearborn marshes. Sperlich also got his hands on an old garage in Michigan Avenue. This was where they were going to play mechanics!

It was not ideal, but Sperlich didn't care. He was in a hurry and willing to put up with anything, so long as he could push ahead. The objectives had been established with Ford and Iacocca. He went over them for the benefit of his team.

'We have just one starting point, one example: the Fiat 127. Our job is to produce a prototype in the same class, but to be competitive it must be better, because we are arriving later. And above all, the direct production cost must be 100 dollars less than that of the Escort. They all think it's impossible. We have to prove otherwise.'

As Sperlich saw it, his first task was to develop a 'concept car' and lay down the ways to achieve it. His approach was eminently pragmatic and systematic. To start with, he brought in from Europe and Japan all the competing models; in all, during the ensuing nine months, nearly thirty cars were taken to pieces and stripped down to the last nut and bolt. Fiat 127 and 128, Renault 5, Honda 600 and Civic, Toyota Publica, Datsun Cherry, Austin Mini, and the Ford Escort and Pinto.

The Ford principle is quite simple: whether they are setting up teams of specialists dealing with experimental work or production methods, whether they are analysing costs or predicting specific production expenses, each car is always regarded as a series of 'sub systems'. In all, fourteen such sub systems are defined, ranging from the bodywork to the electrical system, taking in engine, suspension, transmission, brakes, clutch, steering, exhaust, etc. Each of these sub systems is again divided into a number of components.

At each stage in the evolution of a model, from the preliminary studies to its production, each sub system would thus be handled by groups of specialists. The first to take over in the operation which was now mounted by Hal Sperlich was the team directed by Austin Schimmel.

Schimmel was a real old hand. He ran a group of about 130 cost analysis experts. They were both engineers and accountants, able to judge the quality of a component, the most efficient way to produce it, and what it would cost. They had

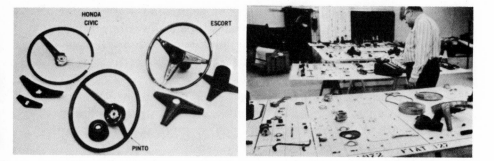

Stripped, measured, analysed, components from competing models helped set targets and objectives for Bobcat planners.

learned all branches of the business at first hand. The least experienced of them had moved from one department to another in the company, from finance to manufacturing, for not less than ten to fifteen years. These were the men who day after day took apart the cars produced by Ford's competitors, estimating to the last quarter of a cent the cost of a bolt from Chevrolet or a nut from Chrysler and then setting the targets for weight and cost of an equivalent item from Ford. But this time it was no longer a duel between Ford and General Motors. They were now taking on the rest of the world.

Schimmel's men stripped down every one of the European and Japanese cars produced for their attention. Every piece was weighed, measured, analysed, photographed, and ticketed. Part by part, sub assembly by sub assembly, the corresponding components of the various models were laid out side by side on large scaled boards, 8 ft long and 4 ft wide, so that direct visual comparisons could be made. The items on each board were numbered, listed, photographed.

Then the judging started. They knew all the rules by heart and all the parameters in the tablets of the law: the quality standards, the rigorous criteria for durability, the targets for weight and cost. They were the ones to choose between the various components brought in for their appraisal; condemning this one because it weighed too much, awarding that one the prize for durability, arriving finally at an order of merit for all the comparable components under two headings, weight and cost.

These, after all, were the great enemies, the two culprits on which they had to pass judgment: excessive weight and abnormal cost. And these were the men, Schimmel's analysts, who finally told the experimental engineers:

'Here are your specific objectives within the framework of the overall target. We will allocate you a budget of two dollars for this component and fifteen cents for that one. If you spend too much here, you will have to make it up by saving somewhere else. But we know that this one should not cost more than two dollars and that one no more than fifteen cents. This is what we think about the parts that make up the cars of the competition, their weight and their cost of production. You be the referees, you find the better ways.'

The arbitration was made by the method of the 'best ball'. When an expert golfer meets several others of lesser strength, one of the ways they can play a game together consists in only computing into the final score the best of the opposing balls on every hole. The automobile business in Detroit is often run like a game of golf. One by one, they take all the balls played by the opposition and they choose the best, the cheapest, the lightest, but also the most ingenious and the most durable, to set the standards for the ball that they must play themselves.

*

However, the approach had to be somewhat different this time. As the primary objective was to save 100 dollars on the Escort production cost, they were not searching for absolute and abstract data. Everything was related to Escort costs when trying to arrive, by a series of successive approximations, at estimates and then detailed objectives which those who were to create this car and perhaps who were going to produce it would have to meet.

'You want to be 100 dollars under the Escort?' said Schimmel's men. 'If you pick the best possible ball, then you will have to save one dollar on the cooling system, seven dollars on the windows, four dollars on the interior lighting.'

But they had not yet arrived at this point during the early autumn days of 1972, when Detroit was still baking under the late sunshine. To translate Schimmel's estimates into practical terms they had to set on foot a foolproof communications system between the analysts and technicians at Dearborn on the one hand, and their counterparts at Merkenich and Dunton on the other hand. Just as five years earlier it had been necessary to teach the two sides of the Channel to speak the same financial and technical language to integrate Ford-Werke and Ford of Britain under the banner of Ford-Europe, the personnel in 'PPR' now had to move forward step by step to integrate the systems of the company on a worldwide basis.

From October, 1972, this became the particular responsibility of Bob Blank, who had been transferred from the financial staff with the task of translating the sparse data available on the programme into clear industrial and accounting objectives.

'We must adopt all the European technical definitions and working methods,' Blank decided, 'not just to give ourselves the pleasure of speaking a common language but so that the whole programme can be switched to Europe as soon as we have finished, and used over there without any trouble.'

And so the coming and going began between Detroit and Europe; experimental engineers, cost analysts, technicians, and accountants arrived from Cologne and London, their briefcases stuffed with files to explain their systems of cost analysis, their manufacturing methods, their rates of pay. Even though they spoke the same language, English, and used the same unit of account, the dollar, everything had to be translated into the same concepts and terms.

Henry Ford said later: 'Nothing but Bobcat could have taught us so well and so quickly all that we have learned from this programme for the benefit of our whole organisation.'

In the beginning the future car had been referred to as *The Deutschlander*, the German. Sperlich lost no time in choosing a more usable name for his operation. Reickert made five or six different suggestions. Sperlich liked 'Bobcat', the name of a wild animal, a sturdily built, fast moving lynx which still haunts the north American forests.

'Next door, in Design, they give their projects the names of flowers' said Sperlich one day. 'Over in Europe, their design studies have feminine names. In Australia, they go for trees. But we're going to use the name of an animal. Something powerful which sticks in the mind and will fire people's imagination. Something that starts with B, like B car. What would you say to Bobcat? Not bad, eh? Bobcat. Right, that's it. We'll call it Bobcat.'

The date was 2 October 1972. Three days later a superb photograph of a lynx was hung above Hal Sperlich's desk.

*

In its early stages, though, the wild cat mostly resembled the Fiat 127. The Italian car had been dissected and analysed piece by piece. They liked the concept, even though they had found some aspects to criticise. This was the car which would serve as a general guide to the members of the Sperlich team, and above all, it was to help them create their first physical pre-prototypes.

Because Ford had never yet built a mini car, they had neither a chassis on which a styling study could be mounted, nor a body which could be used to clothe an experimental chassis. The Fiat 127 therefore had to serve a dual purpose. Its platform and mechanical sub assemblies were used by the designers in Gene Bordinat's styling studios and by those working for Alessandro de Tomaso in Turin. Onto them they grafted their first experimental bodies, those of the 'Mini-Mites' in Detroit and that of the 'Blue Car' at Ghia. Conversely, the first original mechanical assemblies produced by the technical team under Fred Piziali were tested under a Fiat 127.

By now the team was making very rapid progress. Sperlich had got Don della Rosa to order a styling study from Ghia. It was primarily intended to crystallise certain ideas and to supplement the thinking of the Bobcat team. Tom Tjaarda in Turin was a fast worker. He was an American, 36 years old, and the son of a famous Ford designer, but he had spent the most important part of his career in various Turin styling studios before taking charge of operations at Ghia under the control of De Tomaso. In practice Ghia had now become an annexe of the Design Centre at Dearborn, with the enormous advantage that Ghia can create a new body in half the time that it takes in Detroit.

Tjaarda delivered his first version of the Bobcat a mere fifty-three working days after receiving the order from Detroit. It was built upon a Fiat platform but the body and the interior design owed nothing to any other car. Tjaarda and his team had respected the wishes expressed by Sperlich who wanted them to produce a car with a shapely plunging bonnet which

The 'blue car' was built at Ghia in 53 days.

would offer the best possible driving vision. Their prototype, 3 m 50 long, was a little shorter than the Fiat (3 m 59), and space was somewhat restricted in the rear seats, but it was so beautifully executed from the aesthetic point of view that it filled top management, Henry Ford and Lee Iacocca alike, with enthusiasm, while Sperlich and his men were ecstatic.

The 'Blue Car' could not have looked better with its angular front end merging into rounded curves at the rear. A wide transverse moulding extended for the full width of the bonnet. The car was finished in an elegant metallic midnight blue, it had a third door at the rear, and the interior was trimmed in a blue and black tartan fabric.

Iacocca, a great admirer of the Fiat 127 and Henry Ford who preferred the Renault 5 were both sold on this attempt.

'You're on the right track,' they told Sperlich. 'Carry on as fast as you can.'

The prototypes produced by Bordinat were not bad either. Where Tjaarda had taken a few liberties with the dimensions in order to achieve his effect, Bordinat had been more controlled, but also more conventional. His two Mini-Mites, like Tjaarda's car, were equal in length to the Renault 5 (3 m 50) but the lines of their fiberglass bodies were closer to those of the Fiat 127. One of them had front-wheel drive, the other was a conventional rear-wheel drive construction.

These three styling studies were to go places. No sooner were they finished than they were loaded into a freight plane and despatched to Europe, for it was in Europe that they were to be used first in what was to be the most complete and most extensive piece of market research ever conducted in the history of the automobile.

WEEKEND IN LAUSANNE

From the month of October, 1972, even before all the pre-prototypes were available, a team had begun work to establish the basis for a preliminary essay in market research. Henry Ford and Lee Iacocca could not bear to lose a minute. They wanted to find out as quickly as possible what the reactions of the public were to cars in the Bobcat class before the technical part of the pre-programme had a chance to get bogged down in solutions which might turn out to be unrealistic.

There was no time to lose. Before Christmas, Henry Ford wanted to have precise answers to a number of questions on which all the rest would depend. For the first time, the market research specialists received their instructions directly from the twelfth floor, that of the High Command itself. It was no longer simply a question of getting the public reaction to a selection of pre-prototypes, but of obtaining indisputable answers to a certain number of fundamental questions: the importance of front-wheel drive, the commercial potential of Bobcat as a world car, the sales appeal of a third door and the effect that the launching of a new small car would have on sales of the Escort.

In Europe, work had then started under the direction of Bill Bourke on a rejuvenated Escort, which was given the code name of Brenda. It was to be launched at the beginning of 1975. It was essential, before moving on beyond the preliminary studies which had been made for Bobcat, to find out what effect the addition of a new small car to the Ford range would be likely to have on the new Escort. It was no less important to find out whether a cut-down Escort, using nothing but existing mechanical components might not be sufficient to solve the B Car problems. In fact, a sub-Escort was already in preparation at Dunton and Merkenich under the name of Cheetah.

The market research team led by Norman Krandall had only four weeks to draw up their plan of campaign and compose their questionnaire. Krandall got down to business with Jim McKinnon and John Tighe, whose job it would be to co-ordinate research in Europe and South America.

The budget which had been placed at their disposal was impressive. The full range of market investigations undertaken for the whole Bobcat programme was to cost nearly 1,300,000 dollars. This must surely have been the most complete, far-ranging, and costly piece of market research ever undertaken for a consumer product of any kind, whether by Ford or by any of their competitors.

The philosophy behind the whole operation, like that in other fields where Ford is engaged, was founded upon a few simple principles. In the first place, every risk must be reduced to the minimum, and action must always be based on the soundest and safest information. And then, enough money must be spent to establish, if not absolute certainties, at least probabilities which admit of little argument *before* getting irrevocably committed. In this way one insures against the far more serious losses which could later result from a wrong decision. It is the safest way to maximise the gains when the production programme has finally been approved and is eventually set in motion.

*

McKinnon and Tighe left for London in November. Tom Moulson, in charge of market research in Europe, had selected five specialist organizations, in Germany, France, Italy, England and Spain. The original plan was to hold a series of 'clinics' in each of the five countries where a selection of viewers chosen from among potential B-cars buyers would be able to pass judgment on the 'Blue Car' designed in Turin and the 'Mini-Mites' built in Detroit, in comparison with several competing cars already on sale in European markets.

But this would have taken too long. There was no longer time to lug these various prototypes all round Europe if the market research team were to deliver a first series of conclusions to Detroit before the holidays. The only way to go was to organize a single clinic at one central, easily accessible point, and to take there, during one or two weekends, the 700 or so 'judges' who had been engaged in the five countries.

'It's never been done. It's crazy, but it might work,' said one of those responsible as they sat round a conference table in London.

The directors of the market research organizations from five countries which had been mobilised for the occasion were all there. McKinnon explained the situation.

'First of all we must be clearly agreed on what we are trying to do. The whole programme must be perfectly integrated in spite of the language differences and anything else which may set one of your countries apart from the others. We must work as a team, using absolutely identical standards of judgment. Here is what we are going to do...'

Working ten hours a day for a week, these men drawn from the most diverse backgrounds set on foot a market research operation on a continental scale. Each of the concerns involved was to select a hundred potential buyers of small cars by means of door-to-door interviews. The sample had to be completely representative and rigorous standards were laid down to guarantee that it would be.

But before starting this selection, they had to translate and adapt into four other languages the detailed questionnaire which had been compiled in English under the supervision of Norm Krandall. The problem was to respect the spirit of the questions scrupulously, avoiding like the plague the pitfalls of translation. The Spaniard, a former United Nations official, understood each of the other four languages; his wife happened to be an expert in German. The translations were undertaken collectively, its traps were foiled, every word, every question was carefully weighed.

When the questionnaire, the basic tool of the enquiry, was ready at last, and even before the venue for the clinic had been finally decided, they had to make sure that the people selected would consent to make the trip. In the United States, the participants in a clinic of this kind each receive a sum of 10 to 15 dollars in return for their trouble. A poll taken among a hundred Londoners showed that 80 per cent of them would be willing to take part in a clinic in their own city, and at least the same number would be prepared to accept a 24-hour trip to a foreign town. No falling off in numbers was therefore to be feared on this account and there was no reason why the organization of a single clinic should not go ahead. Each participant was to be given five dollars purely to cover incidental expenses, as the attraction of a brief tourist trip abroad was regarded as a sufficient reward for the effort that was to be expected of them. Examining the cars and providing the answers to the questionnaire would take round about two hours per person.

*

But where was the clinic to be held? The city chosen must be easily accessible by air and it must possess a large exhibition hall, sufficiently well protected to permit everything to be run in the strictest secrecy, under cover from prying cameras.

John Tighe and Tom Moulson visited several possible sites. Finally, they chose Lausanne and its Palais de Beaulieu, a group of spacious buildings intended for large and comprehensive exhibitions, a part of which could be reserved for the Bobcat operation. A kitchen was placed at their disposal and a contract was set up with a caterer who was to provide refreshment, solid and liquid. A fleet of buses was also reserved to take charge of the travellers from the moment they arrived at the Cointrin airport at Geneva. While one group would be driven to Lausanne to look at the cars, another would be taken for a coach tour. Radio transmitters and receivers were installed in the coaches and at the headquarters in the Palais de Beaulieu, for communications had to be instantaneous and precise, so that as soon as one group finished their work and moved out to take their outing along the edge of the lake and through the vineyards of the Vaud and the Valais, another could be brought in to take their place.

Potential customers carefully selected in five European countries pass judgment on the first Ford 'concept cars' compared with competing models. The conclusions of this research greatly influenced the final decisions of Ford's engineers and designers.

Great care had to be taken to ensure that two groups from different countries never met, and that each group found its appropriate national environment on arrival: signs and identification cards in their own language, the appropriate questionnaires and an adequate staff to look after them; Spaniards to explain the procedure to the Spaniards, French staff to help the French, Germans to interpret the questionnaires for the German visitors.

*

In Düsseldorf, London, Paris, Milan and Madrid, each of the market research organisations taking part in the operation selected its hundred B Car prospects. These five hundred people were joined by two hundred others chosen in the same countries from owners or potential buyers of Escorts. The latter had but one task, that of evaluating the Bobcat pre-prototypes in comparison with the Escort itself, a preliminary operation which was to be supplemented some months later in England and Italy by a confrontation between the Bobcat and the Cheetah, the prototype of a shortened Escort.

The operation was not without its complications. The people who were invited to make the trip were simply told that they would spend 24 hours in Lausanne to take part in an automotive marketing investigation. In no circumstances were they ever to know that the operation was being conducted by Ford. In Paris, the husband of one of the young ladies approached by the organizers called the police.

'Someone has been trying to kidnap my wife,' he stormed. 'There's a gang setting up a white slave organisation.'

The vice squad immediately started enquiries. They got in touch with all the car manufacturers—including Ford France—to try to find out which of them might have mounted such an operation. But no one had any clues; not even the management of the French subsidiary concerned, as secrecy had been maintained to the point of saying nothing at all to Ford's various national branches. The French police eventually closed their investigations without ever learning the point of the whole affair.

Another young Parisienne confronted the organizers with a rather different problem. At the end of the clinic she refused to return to France, announcing that she had no intention of going back to her husband. They got her to sign an indemnity and the plane left Geneva without her.

One of the Londoners thanked his guides for the excellent day he had spent in their company: 'I've always dreamed of visiting *Sweden*. It was great,' he said, convinced that he had been taken on a tour of Stockholm, and not on the shores of Lake Geneva.

The visit of the German group was naturally organised with typical Teutonic thoroughness. The chosen visitors from Düsseldorf were the first to arrive on the very first day, full of ardour and enthusiasm. Their guides had thought of everything, provided for every eventuality; except that they had left all the questionnaires behind in the aeroplane!

*

The clinic was held during the first two weekends of December, 1972. Seven unidentified cars were presented to the test prospects, uniformly painted white to avoid any possibility that different colours might influence their judgment: a Fiat 127, a Renault 5, a Peugeot 104, a Honda Civic, the experimental car evolved by De Tomaso and two Mini-Mites, externally similar but differing in their interior accommodation, one having front-wheel drive and the other being of conventional construction.

In this first phase of the enquiry the main object was to assess the reactions of European B Car buyers to a certain number of aesthetic and functional characteristics. Bobcat had to be judged in relation to the current stars on the European market but it was even more important to obtain an order of preference between the three cars which had been brought over from Detroit.

On style and appearance the verdict favoured Ford. Each car was given points from one to ten and the Mini-Mite came out on top with 7.1 points ahead of the De Tomaso (7.0), the Peugeot 104 (6.6), the Honda Civic (6.5), the Fiat 127 (6.2), and the Renault 5 (6.2). Going into more detail, the public preferred the front of the Italian prototype, but the sides and rear of the American model.

The combined verdicts on the comfort and interior space produced equal marks for the De Tomaso, the front-drive Mini-Mite, the Fiat 127 and the Peugeot 104, each with 6.7 points. But the rear-drive Mini-Mite became a casualty with 5.8. The opinion of these five samples representing the European motoring public thus confirmed the judgment of the technicians in giving absolute preference to front-wheel drive.

Some months later this preference was to appear still more clearly in the comparison between the De Tomaso prototype and the Cheetah. The latter, an economical solution consisting of a shortened Escort, was beaten all along the line; on external appearance, comfort, interior space, and the size of the luggage boot.

A first series of rough conclusions thus arrived on the desks of Ford, Iacocca, and the planning technicians shortly before the year end holidays. While digesting their Christmas turkey, these gentlemen had every opportunity to ponder the two points which stood out most clearly. One of them was very satisfying: the styling of their pre-prototypes was clearly preferable in the eyes of the European public to that of the two current best sellers on the market, the Fiat 127 and the Renault 5. The other, although incontrovertible, was none the less disagreeable. It put them under an obligation to take a road virtually unknown at Ford—if one excepts a rather unhappy experience with the old Taunus 12M—, that of front-wheel drive. A road paved with problems, technical, industrial and financial.

The front and rear-wheel drive Mini-Mites, as presented to the 700 'judges' assembled in Lausanne in December 1972.

MINI MITE

The Krandall-McKinnon team worked flat out during the holidays so as to be able to deliver by the end of January a more detailed report which was to prove an exceptionally useful working guide for the designers and technicians. The multitude of questions which had been asked brought in a rich harvest of precise and readily usable answers indicating the preferences of potential buyers.

Apart from the technical factors which emerged, various considerations of an economic nature gave encouragement to the Ford researchers. First of all, it was clear that if faced with a definite decision to buy a car, the Lausanne guinea pigs declared a 56 per cent interest in the De Tomaso prototype and the front-drive Mini-Mite, against 55 per cent in the Fiat 127, 51 per cent in the rear-drive Mini-Mite, but only 48 per cent in the Renault 5, 45 per cent in the Honda Civic and 41 per cent in the Peugeot 104.

Moreover, when they were told the price of the Fiat 127 as a point of reference, the Lausanne visitors estimated that the front-drive Mini-Mite would cost 4 per cent more, and the De Tomaso 2 per cent more. Conversely, they throught the Renault 5 should cost 8 per cent less.

In addition, the panel expressed very clear technical preferences. Although they were informed in the questionnaires that rear drive, drum brakes and a rigid rear axle would cost respectively 39, 44 and 39 dollars less than front drive, disc brakes and independent rear suspension, they chose the dearer and more sophisticated solutions in the proportions of 71, 85 and 74 per cent, explaining their preference by considerations of comfort, efficiency and safety, thus revealing a sharp perception of the technical facts of life on the part of the average European buyer.

On the basis of the collected answers, Ford's researchers constructed a theoretical extrapolation to determine the global commercial potential of Bobcat and the specific potential of a front-wheel drive model compared with a conventional car. Taking a theoretical annual Bobcat production of 260,000 units, they concluded that 160,000 would represent extra or 'conquest' sales and 100,000 would be 'substitution' sales gained at the expense of the Escort. With a Bobcat production of 460,000, the new sales would be 340,000 units and the substitution sales only 120,000. But if rear-wheel drive was chosen, this would reduce the extra sales by anything from 25,000 to 40,000 units in the first hypothesis and by 50,000 to 85,000 in the second.

*

For those who conceived it, Bobcat had never been regarded as an exclusively European car. Certainly no one yet foresaw the energy crisis, but some of them were already dreaming of turning the new model into a world car. This was to be carried out in three steps. In phase one, the car would be built in Europe only, with engines imported from Brazil. Phase two called for construction in Brazil also from where it was to be exported to the US. The third possible step was assembly of Bobcat in North America. Finally, a fourth step could be the making of the car in the Asia-Pacific area. Whatever would happen later, it was therefore important in any case to test out its potential elsewhere than in Europe.

The three experimental cars had no sooner returned to Detroit by air freight than two of them were in the air again, the De Tomaso and the rear-drive Mini-Mite. Their first stop was at San Mateo in California, where in January, 1973, an American clinic comparable with the Lausanne exercise was held. Lined up this time with two versions of the Bobcat were a Fiat 127, a VW Beetle, and a Ford Pinto, the most compact of the American Fords. Seven hundred prospects in all stood in line to look at these five cars: 200 foreign car buyers, 200 owners of American 'sub compacts', 100 potential first-car buyers, 100 heads of two-car or three-car families and 100 potential buyers of used cars.

Overall the Pinto and the Beetle came out ahead of the two Fords, which in turn were ahead of the Fiat 127. It was especially on external appearance that the experimental cars received poor marks. Confirming the judgment of the Europeans, the Californian panel expressed a clear preference for front-wheel drive; on the score of comfort and interior space, the De Tomaso prototype came out ahead of all the other cars present, even including the Pinto.

This result was considered sufficient to justify the total abandonment of rear-wheel drive before the third in this series of clinics was held at São Paulo in February. En route for Brazil, the two front-drive experimental cars made a detour to Florida, where they were shown to a group of about 150 Ford senior executives assembled at Boca Raton. Those present at this meeting found some faults with the cars, but in the main they were enthusiastic. The 'pre-advanced' research programme was far from finished, but already the project was moving on the right lines. In Detroit, even the most sceptical had begun to believe in it.

*

And now for Brazil! To save time, they were going to obtain the opinions of the Brazilian and the Argentinian markets simultaneously by bringing a hundred carefully selected Argentines in from Buenos Aires for the weekend. This time the Ford researchers were anxious to organise their South American clinic at Rio. Krandall's analysts had very unhappy memories of a previous clinic held at São Paulo. Down there it was apparently impossible to keep any secrets at all. The very next day a local daily paper, *Estado*, had devoted four pages, including its front page, to pictures taken surreptitiously during the clinic.

Krandall's men had firmly decided not to set foot in São Paulo again and above all, not to unload their prototypes there. Unfortunately for them, Rio was preparing for the Carnival and no suitable site could be found at the foot of the Sugar Loaf mountain. Come what may, they must go to São Paulo, but this time they took some quite exceptional and expensive precautions. They even went so far as to invite all the motoring journalists of São Paulo to go on a visit to the Ford factories in Detroit and then on to the European factories to make sure that they were far away from base for ten days so that the clinic could be organised in their absence without the risk of leakage!

The presentation of the cars was held in an unused building in the centre of the city, which had formerly been a repair depot for trucks. Everything was re-painted, even the floor, and potted plants were brought in to liven up the decor. For the benefit of the Brazilian panel, the front-drive Bobcats were opposed by the Fiat 127 (at that time unknown in Argentina and Brazil), the VW Beetle and the Ford Corcel, a Brazilian version of the Renault 12 which had been conceived before Renault sold their factory there to Ford. Being roomier—in fact it was a C Class car—the Corcel won hands down, but the front-drive Mini-Mite was a good second.

The scenery was changed again for the Argentine guinea pigs; this time the front-drive Mini-Mite was the only one of the Ford experimental cars on view and it was confronted by a selection of Argentine best sellers: the Dodge 1500, the Fiat 600 and 128 and the inevitable Fiat 127. As cars of a higher class, the 128 and the Dodge came out on top, mainly because of their larger interior space and their greater luggage capacity, but the Mini-Mite was close on their heels so far as external appearance was concerned and, which was most important, it was clearly ahead of the Fiat 127.

The South American studies confirmed the previous ones. Even in the form of a rough first attempt, the Bobcat was a competitive product worldwide and seemed capable of doing better than the Fiat 127, the model used as a standard, on all the markets examined, with the exception of Italy, where the little car from Turin was naturally the favourite.

In all the eight countries considered, the Fiat 127 was given the best marks for the space available for luggage, which led Ford's engineers to make a special effort in this direction. On the score of apparent comfort and interior space, the overall result was a draw which was scarcely surprising, considering that the experimental Fords were built on Fiat 127 chassis. Bobcat was preferred by the British, the Spaniards, and the Californians. The Germans, Italians, Brazilians, and Argentines preferred the Fiat. The French gave equal marks to Ford and Fiat.

It was under the heading of external appearance that Bobcat came out well ahead of all the others: seven countries out of eight rated it the best; only Italy chose the Fiat and then by a tiny margin.

*

A number of questions remained to be resolved, but the movement was now advancing on all fronts. In Detroit the Bobcat designers began working overtime to get their first complete pre-prototypes finished. The marketing specialists prepared to launch the second wave of their enquiries in five European countries. Finally, Dick Holmes was rapidly turning into a Spaniard...

A rear view of the Mini-Mite: the public preferred front wheel drive.

AN EAGLE FOR SPAIN

Every Monday or just about, a tall, heavy, jovial, 40 year-old fair haired man—the shoulders of a rugby player clad in a business suit—arrived at dawn at Stansted airport in England's home counties. This was the place from where Spitfires took off for the European mainland during the war.

The jet engines of the Hawker Siddeley 125 were already whistling away as Dick Holmes heaved his weight on board. The Ford-Europe executive jet was his whenever he wanted it. His mission had top priority. It was also top secret. The high command of Ford Europe had given it a code name: Eagle.

'Let's go!' said Holmes, and the small white, orange, and blue jet turned on to the runway.

The Eagle which rose into the sky in the thin light of these early mornings, always heading in the same direction, had nothing in common with the majestic bird of prey which symbolises the United States of America. This Eagle was interested in only one quarry, Spain.

*

Spain was a private preserve. Five manufacturers shared the market between them: SEAT (an associate of Fiat), Renault, Citroen, Authi (which assembled British Leyland models), and Barreiros (a subsidiary of Chrysler). There was no way to sell vehicles in Spain except to build them on the spot; strict regulations provided that the local content of a Spanish car must be equivalent to 95 per cent of its value.

Ford had already made several attempts to establish themselves beyond the Pyrenees. Talks had been held about a possible purchase of the Authi assembly plants at Pamplona, and the truck factories of Aissa, but they came to nothing. Ford had also made a proposition to the government which involved building a factory to make mechanical components. The parts manufactured there would have been exported to other European plants of the group and in return Ford would have been authorised to import parts to assemble 10,000 to 20,000 cars a year in Spain for sale on the local market. This proposal had aroused no interest whatever on the part of the Spanish government.

Some people had even suggested to Holmes that he should look into the possibility of buying Barreiros from Chrysler as at that time the enterprise was losing between ten and fifteen million dollars a year.

'None of this is of any use to us,' said Holmes to Henry Ford. 'There aren't six and thirty ways to get ourselves established in Spain. There is only one. Set up our own assembly plant complete, press shop, body build, and final assembly.'

'Sure, but you know what we need before we can do that!'

Holmes knew exactly. The Spanish legislation then in force raised almost insurmountable obstacles for any manufacturer who wanted to get in and join the five already established on the Iberian peninsula.

First obstacle: no foreign company was allowed to own more than 50 per cent of the capital of any Spanish company. Now, just when they were pushing ahead with the maximum integration of their operations in Europe, if not yet throughout the world, Ford could not possibly accept being a minority shareholder in a company as important as the one they had in mind for Spain. It was not solely a matter of principle but also a practical problem. When the various elements constituting a car had to come from widely scattered sources—Ford engines coming perhaps from England, Ford transmissions from Bordeaux, suspensions possibly built in Germany—it was hardly possible to contemplate a situation where the group would not also have control of the factories at the end of the line which would make the finished product. Ford likes things to be simple and clear-cut. It is always best to avoid complications. Any partnership in Spain would be a source of difficulties.

The second obstacle, naturally, was the Madrid government's stipulation that a car built in Spain must be 95 per cent Spanish, which implied that practically all its components, including the engine and transmission must be made in Spanish territory.

The third problem was that of the rates of customs duty to be levied on the parts imported from outside Spain. With the rate then standing at 30 per cent Ford felt it would be impossible to achieve competitive manufacture in Spain even if the first two obstacles could be removed. When Dick Holmes found himself face to face for the first time with Lopez de Letona, the Minister for Industry, he had however one exceptionally powerful weapon in his armoury.

'If you amend your legislation', he promised, 'we are prepared to embark on a major project; big enough to build about 225,000 cars a year in Spain, two-thirds of which would be exported.'

'That's interesting. Very interesting,' said the Minister.

At that time the whole Spanish industry did not produce more than 450,000 cars in a year, more than half of them being built by SEAT; exports were merely nominal. At a stroke, Ford would be giving Spain a completely new industrial dimension and thus enabling it to gain a firm footing in European markets.

The idea that Holmes was developing was based on the projections which Ford had made on future volumes of production. It appeared, in effect, that if Ford produced the Escort and Taunus in Spain, they would hope to sell some 60,000 to 80,000 units a year on the Spanish market from 1976 onwards, that is, 8 to 9 per cent of the total new car registrations. At the same time, provided they could be produced at a competitive cost, these cars could be exported to France and Italy at the rate of 125,000 to 150,000 units a year. Total, 200,000 to 230,000 cars, almost the ideal production volume for a standard assembly plant.

'We could make Spain our springboard for Southern Europe, for all the Latin countries,' Holmes explained to Lopez de Letona. 'Obviously we could wait until Spain joins the Common Market as you contemplate. Your barriers would then disappear automatically. But if we are to do something before then, we shall have to remove a number of obstacles created by your regulations.'

'Very well, Mr Holmes, let us have a look at these obstacles and see what we can do about them.'

*

For two long years these negotiations continued; long, difficult, but always cordial, because both parties wanted them to succeed. On the Spanish side the principal spokesman was a high official of the Ministry for Industry, Carlos Perez de Bricio. An indefatigable worker and a tough and uncompromising negotiator who rarely betrayed what he was thinking, De Bricio was a worthy opponent for Holmes. The two men were in for quite some wrestling! Holmes was assisted by a young lawyer from Madrid, Antonio Garrigues Walker, who was equally at home among the complex industrial problems of great multi-national corporations and the arcana of Madrid's legal and political world. His father had been Spanish ambassador to Washington in the days of President Kennedy. Completely bi-lingual he was a personal friend of Henry Ford and one of the few men in the whole world who addressed him by his first name.

Garrigues was thus able on several occasions to call for the personal intervention of Henry Ford. At his request, Ford would fly over to Madrid to hold top level talks, and ratify the agreements which were concluded one by one with the government representatives. Eagle was very much Henry Ford's personal project. He more than anyone resented his company's absence in the Mediterranean. Southern Europe is his second fatherland. He wanted to feel at home there professionally just as he already did in the personal sense. Every month, Holmes sent him a private report and on all his visits to Europe, three or four times a year, Ford's first priority was catching up with the situation in Spain.

80

After clearing the ground with Dick Holmes, Carlos Perez de Bricio would report to his Minister. He in turn made recommendations to his colleagues in the government who dealt with finance, economic affairs, and labour, obtained their opinions and asked for their agreement before getting the new measures ratified by the Council of Ministers.

The idea which emerged little by little was to define a statute for 'Companies of Preferential Interest.' These would be corporations capable of making an exceptional contribution to the Spanish economy and would be required to meet a number of precise industrial and commercial objectives. In return, new regulations would be introduced to assist their operations.

Agreement was first reached on the rights of ownership accorded to foreign companies. At the end of 1971 the Spanish government accepted that, under certain conditions, Ford and other companies who came into the same category should be permitted 100 per cent control of their Spanish subsidiaries. This decision removed one of the three original obstacles.

'We have made some progress,' Dick Holmes reported to London. 'Up to now they allowed us 49 per cent of a disaster. Now we have the right to 100 per cent of a catastrophe!'

To avoid such trouble, one reform was now essential; a reduction in the compulsory percentage of local content. This was an affair of state. It was all the more difficult to negotiate because the manufacturers already operating in Spain, who had gone to the trouble and expense of building fully integrated factories there, were naturally vigorously opposed to the arrival of a new competitor who would not be subject to the same strict regulations.

Nevertheless, the prospect of welcoming a new manufacturer who would not only create a considerable number of new jobs in Spain, but would also undertake to re-export the greater part of his production, was so attractive that the Madrid government could not fail to adapt the existing legislation to the new circumstances. Even so, months went by before a solution emerged.

This happened before the end of 1972, and it gave Ford what they hoped for while fully protecting the interests of the manufacturers already established in Spain. The decree, which was officially promulgated in December, provided that a 'Company of Preferential Interest' coming to establish itself in Spain in conformity with the new regulations must strictly limit its sales in Spain to 10 per cent of the market total for the previous year; 70,000 units for example if 700,000 had been sold during the preceding year. Further, every company wishing to have the benefit of the new legislation must re-export at least two-thirds of its production.

In return for these undertakings, the proportion of local content required in a car was officially brought down to 50 per cent. But in practice this figure rose to 66 per cent because the decree laid down that the company could bring in imports up to 50 per cent of the value of its exports. Since two-thirds of production was to be exported, one could bring in imports equivalent to half of this value, i.e. one third of the overall value of the finished product, the remaining two thirds being entirely Spanish.

These proportions, although relatively onerous, were none the less acceptable to Ford. Holmes returned to London to report his success to the management of Ford-Europe.

'It's fixed.' he exulted, 'We can go! With 66 per cent of local content, we have what we need, a complete assembly plant with press shop, body build, final assembly. And we can import our mechanical assemblies. 250,000 units a year. It'll work.'

'No so fast, Dick, not so fast! Are you really sure that we're going to be competitive? Have you gone into the costs of production?'

'Well...'

'Remember one thing. With the deal you have now, you are going to pay 30 per cent customs duties on everything you import. Now, you are proposing to import one third of the value of the vehicles.'

'Er...'

'Dick, you must have another go. Look at it again. In theory the law now permits us to manufacture in Spain in the way we want. But it won't stand up financially. Our production costs will be too high. We shall not be competitive.'

So Holmes climbed back into his jet, met de Bricio at the Ministry for Industry, re-opened the discussions, set forth his arguments. The Minister hesitated. This time it was the Spanish component manufacturers who raised objections. They felt very well protected in the shelter of the customs duties. What Holmes was asking for was nothing less than a deep breach in this protective wall.

In the end the long-term national interest would still prevail with the Spanish government. To pave the way for their entry into the Common Market—they had already sent observers to Brussels—Spain must at once broaden its industrial base and establish a position in export markets. The Ford project could save Spain several years. The factories which the giant from Detroit had promised would create several thousand new jobs. Thousands of new jobs also for the sub-contractors. New techniques would be introduced. And there would be a flood of foreign currency pouring in from the sale of the cars which were exported to the rest of Europe.

In September, 1972, Madrid gave its verdict. Customs duties on imported components within the limits already defined were reduced from 30 per cent to 5 per cent and a considerable reduction was conceded in the rate of any indispensable machine tools and equipment which could not be obtained in Spain itself.

'Gentlemen,' said Holmes to the Ford-Europe top management, 'this time I really believe that we no longer have a problem. I've got you your factory. Where do you want it?'

'Where do you suggest?' asked Henry Ford.

*

During the two years Dick Holmes had spent commuting week by week between England and Spain—with an occasional detour to Iran, Nigeria, or the Congo, where he and his staff were simultaneously working on other development projects—he visited other places besides the ministries in Madrid.

Accompanied sometimes by an assistant, Arthur Molyneaux, and sometimes by a guide-interpreter, Ken Milner—a young American who had settled in Madrid after marrying a Spanish girl and who, in his spare time, sold cars to the American forces—Holmes had turned into an explorer. If the factory they hoped for was one day to see the light, he might as well find the best site for it. This involved analysing the possibilities offered by the various provinces and the principal cities, getting to know the infrastructure available—roads, railways, port installations, the labour market and the conditions laid down for the establishment of a new factory by the provincial and local authorities.

Holmes had been given a list by the Minister for Industry which showed the cities where the government wished to encourage industrial development. He also visited others which Madrid had not recommended. In quick succession he ruled out Barcelona, the 'Spanish Detroit' where SEAT was operating, and Valladolid where Renault had already absorbed all the available manpower.

Pamplona attracted him. By virtue of an agreement made with the central government in the fifteenth century, the province of Navarra enjoyed special fiscal privileges. These enabled the representative of the local *Deputación*, the provincial council, to offer Ford attractive conditions for setting up business: help with investments, free grants of land and tax reductions. Holmes found the site ideal. He learned that the local university had an excellent relationship with several U.S. universities and that a number of other enterprises of American origin were already established there. Very soon he was as enthusiastic about Pamplona as Ernest Hemingway had been, but for reasons which had rather less to do with bull fighting.

On arriving in the city one morning he learned that a Señor Huarte, a wealthy industrialist, had just been kidnapped by the Basque nationalists and they would only release him on payment of a large ransom.

'Huarte is as big and strong as you are,' they told him in Pamplona. 'We wondered whether it wasn't you they were after!'

Holmes told the story to Philip Caldwell, chairman of Ford-Europe.

'I wasn't at all worried', he said, 'I knew that Ford would pay my ransom. The only thing I was anxious about was that it would have taken so long to get it through the various committees that I'd have been in pretty poor shape by the time I emerged from captivity.'

Ford decided against Pamplona, much to Holmes' regret. Authi was already installed there and John McDougall (responsible for manufacturing and future president of Ford-Europe) feared that the local labour market would not be able to produce the number of employees needed.

So Holmes resumed his travels. He had brought in a Ford 17M from Germany as a temporary import and found a chauffeur to drive it. Starting in the north, he uncovered Santander with its harbour and its mists which reminded him of those of the English countryside, Oviedo, the vineyards of Logrono, Burgos, Saragossa, the orange groves of Castellon, Sagunto where the construction of giant steel works left no room for Ford, and finally, Valencia.

'Other cities further away have also been suggested: Alicante, and further south still, Seville, Cadiz and Algeciras', explained Holmes. 'They are too distant. We would be under heavy handicap with the transport costs. My personal choice would be either Saragossa or Valencia.'

*

Ford did not yet have even the smallest office in Spain. They had nothing but Dick Holmes's car and he had nowhere to stop over except a series of hotel rooms along his way. The Eagle project must be kept secret, more especially because General Motors also seemed to be interested in getting established in Spain.

Nevertheless, Ford technicians began to show their noses. A German public works engineer was seconded to Holmes and Henry Ford's visit to Madrid in February, 1972, did not pass unnoticed in official and industrial circles.

According to the preliminary investigations made by transport specialists who had been drafted from Warley into Spain, Valencia seemed the best bet, with its harbour and its connections by road and rail. Contacts with the local authorities were therefore intensified. Accompanied by Señor Perello, president of the Valencia *Deputación*, Holmes toured the surrounding countryside. Every time he stopped, there was the local mayor offering him oranges by the sackful. That year Holmes' eight children did not go short of vitamin C. This part of Spain was

The Almusafes site before the beginning of construction

86

covered with orange groves, but the economic situation was not very encouraging; oranges were hard to sell because of increasingly fierce competition from producers in North Africa and Israel. Valencia wanted to become a centre of industry. The city arms bear the motto *Ciudad historica y laboriosa*, historical and industrious city. It is celebrated for its flowers and for its toy makers. It also produces furniture, ceramics, shoes, and household equipment. Even so, it needed other activities to provide a living for its 500,000 inhabitants.

ɔme orange groves but mostly fields of onions and artichokes.

'You would be very welcome here,' said Vicente Bosch.

Proprietor of a small agricultural holding, a lean, upright, and vigorous sixty-year-old, Bosch was the mayor of Almusafes, a village of 3,657 souls less than ten miles from the centre of Valencia. The Mediterranean was only three miles away as the crow flies, and there was access to it via a lagoon where the fishermen caught *angullas* and where hunters laid in wait for wild duck. Between the orange groves there were fields of artichokes, onions, and lettuce. Further on, there were some rice fields.

'Look,' said the mayor, 'here, between the road and the railway should suit you nicely.'

Half a mile wide, the site extended for 1.8 miles. In all, nearly 640 acres of agricultural land—the equivalent of 360 football fields! Some of it orange groves (it was calculated later that they occupied about 18 per cent of the total area), but mostly fields of onions and artichokes. It was all in tiny plots, the result of holdings being split up among the heirs on the death of an owner. Holmes would learn later that the land belonged to 636 different owners with whom he would have to negotiate the purchase. On the map, Perello showed him the line of the motorway which was due to by-pass Valencia from 1978 onwards and the access road to Almusafes running along the proposed site.

'Yes', said Holmes 'this would do very well.'

*

At Warley, accountants, economists, planners, and technicians got to work. The final decree of the Spanish government which made the new terms of admission official was not published until 7 December 1972. But the Eagle project for a Ford factory in Spain took a concrete form at the Ford—Europe headquarters in September, when Phil Caldwell the Chairman, supported it before the Operating Policy Committee, the first stage on the road to a discussion at the summit with the members of the board in Detroit.

Earlier in the same year an analysis had been made of Ford's global production potential which forecast that without taking into account any sales in Spain, the output needed from Ford-Europe would rise from 1.4 million units a year in 1972 to 1.5 million in 1975 and 1.8 million in 1982. The first project envisaged to meet these requirements was the extension of the Saarlouis factory in 1976 and 1977, where production would be raised progressively from 930 to 1,330 and eventually 1,670 units a day. The inauguration of a Spanish factory with a production potential of 640 a day theoretically only entered into the plan for 1980.

'Provided that our negotiations with the Spanish government progress quickly and favourably, which seems likely, we propose to bring forward the starting date for a possible Spanish factory by four years,' said Phil Caldwell. 'Production could start in January 1976.'

Bobcat was still but an idea and no one yet knew whether it would ever become a reality, so at that time the only possible production programme for Spain centred on the renovated Escort, then in preparation under the code name of Brenda, and the Taunus.

The project proposed by Caldwell was a press shop and an assembly plant with engines being imported. In Spain itself the objective was to capture 4.4 per cent of the market with Brenda and a similar amount with the Taunus.

The factory envisaged would employ 6,300 people, rising to 7,600 in 1978, when the daily production would have increased from 640 to 930 units.

The theoretical studies went on for several weeks at the headquarters of Ford-Europe. They juggled with the figures, examining the evidence for and against, challenging the assumptions and verifying the facts in the usual way. By the end of 1972 no firm decision had been made, but it was then practically certain that Ford was to become Spanish without further delay. The person most concerned no longer had any doubts. Henry Ford had declared:

'We are going into Spain.'

Their job is to produce design projects for Ford. From left to right, Tjaarda, Head and Sapino, the men in charge at Ghia, Ford's subsidiary in Turin.

ARRIBA BOBCAT!

'I'll give you six months more, Hal, until June. I need your prototype at the beginning of June', said Iacocca.

Henry Ford was leaning on Iacocca and Iacocca was pushing Sperlich. The opening up of Spain drove them to accelerate the work on Bobcat even faster than before. They were not yet talking about it openly, but Ford and Iacocca in Detroit and Caldwell and Bourke in London were thinking secretly of a possible marriage between the bird and the lynx, a merger between projects Eagle and Bobcat. Now that the Eagle was approaching maturity, the Bobcat must not be allowed to lag.

Piece by piece, the experimental engineers defined the components of their concept car. To guide them they had the cost analyses provided by Schimmel's team, the objectives established by the 'best ball' procedure and the weight limits previously defined. Regular commuting went on between Merkenich and Dunton on the one hand and Detroit on the other. Mostly it was by normal airline services, but top management used the company's Grumman Gulfstream II, as fast a jet as any of the commercial flights. Iacocca himself crossed the Atlantic 29 times in four years.

'I wonder how we would build cars if they had not invented airplanes!' remarked Henry Ford ironically.

Engineers were coming and going between Europe and America, comparing ideas, figures and targets. The cooperation which developed between the various experimental departments was not without a certain amount of rivalry but it was a fruitful process.

'You'll never make it!', said one.

'Yes, here's how.'

'Impossible. We've already tried it,' said the other.

'Then let's try again.'

'You'll never save three dollars on that thing!'

'We think we might even save four...'

They were continually struggling to beat the two cars that set the standards: the Escort, most economical car produced by Ford anywhere in the world, compared with which they had to save a hundred dollars in variable production cost and a good deal of weight, and the Fiat 127 the basic concept of which they had to retain while producing something better.

'We shall be just about the last to get started, so we must be the best.'

A slogan symbolized this policy: 'Last in, best out!'

Liaison was established between the experimental engineers now regrouped under the leadership of Fred Piziali, and the purchasing and manufacturing staffs to determine what were the practical possibilities of achieving the concepts they had in mind. Along the way the European engineers working on the Brenda prototype—the new Ford Escort which was to be launched at the beginning of 1975—picked up some of the fruits of this work; what was good for Bobcat could perhaps be good for Brenda too.

Piziali put in hand five different cars. Four were composite prototypes using a Fiat 127 body and a Fiat platform modified to take an original Ford sub assembly—front suspension on one, rear suspension on another, complete engine and transmission on a third, heating, ventilation and electrical system on a fourth. Each of the sub assemblies could thus be tested separately at minimum cost.

The fifth prototype was to be the definitive concept car bringing together all the sub assemblies. This one would owe nothing to Fiat. This would be Bobcat, a pre-prototype created in the record time of nine months, starting with nothing except a car from a competitor.

At De Tomaso's in Turin, Tom Tjaarda had created a new styling study, a yellow coupe to be known as the 'Wolf'; he also offered a more utilitarian version of it. These little wolves, first seen at Merkenich in Germany before crossing the Atlantic, proved even more attractive to Ford's top brass than the

Above: On the Almusafes site in Spain, between some orange groves, from left to right: Hanns Brand, manager of the future factory, Jack Hooven, technical head of Ford Europe, Vicente Bosch, the mayor of Almusafes, and Bill Bourke, president and future chairman of Ford Europe.
Below: On the occasion of the laying of the cornerstone of the Spanish factory, Henry Ford flanked by Phil Caldwell (left), head of Ford's international operations, Bill Bourke, Carl Levy, president of Ford Spain, and Horatio Liberatore, in charge of factory construction.

experimental 'blue car' which had been market tested at Lausanne, San Mateo and São-Paulo.

Wolf was to serve as the basis for the definitive styling study. The idea of the bonnet falling away sharply towards the front was retained, partly for aerodynamic efficiency and also for the superior driving vision in every direction. It was the size of the glass areas more than anything else which distinguished Bobcat, making it seem more modern than all the existing models.

Obviously this car had front-wheel drive; market research and the analysis of competing models had made this choice inevitable, even for those who still harboured unhappy memories of the Taunus 12M or of the stillborn front wheel drive Thunderbird prototype. But they were trying to produce a revolutionary new front suspension using double torsion bars of a completely novel design: U-shaped bars which would act as springs, anti-roll bars and radius arms all in one single piece.

The first trials of this suspension were functionally satisfactory but gave no guarantee of durability. Other tests were set up to look after that. In any case it was worth trying; besides being technically attractive it offered a cost saving of up to five dollars and an appreciable saving in weight—nearly 9lb. As an additional advantage, the space saved by this suspension would allow the spare wheel to be carried under the bonnet, leaving room for an appreciably larger luggage boot at the rear of the car.

The engine of this pre-prototype was the old Kent four-cylinder already used on the Anglia and then the Escort, slightly modified to meet the requirements of front-wheel drive. If a completely new engine was to be called for, Europe would be left to look after it. Once again, this was not a final car that they were endeavouring to create, but a concept car, an advanced sketch. The components of this Bobcat prototype could still be re-arranged, modified or replaced, until perhaps nothing was left of the initial prototype. But from now on they would have to retain the ideas, the new systems, the original concepts and the objectives, whether on cost of production, weight, durability, economy, functional efficiency, simplicity of construction and maintenance, or ease of access to the mechanical parts.

Component by component, function by function, the targets were clearly defined. Taking the Fiat 127 as a basis of comparison, they awarded it a coefficient of 100 which they were content to equal on points such as directional stability, comfort and heating. In other directions they were straining after appreciable improvements; the gear change mechanism for example must rate 110. The same applied to the sound level from the transmission, whereas the ventilation, the screen washers and the direction indicators must rate 105.

Throughout the evolution of the final prototype and right up to the start of production, every part of the car would thus be periodically evaluated in relation to the targets already fixed. Later the arrival of new competitors was to lead to a re-evaluation and frequently a raising of the initial targets. The functional efficiency and quality of the product must improve unceasingly in the process of ripening and perfecting which led from the pre-prototype to the final production model. Only the weight and the production cost expressed in constant economic terms were henceforth immutable.

*

Piziali and his staff were relying mainly on sub contractors. The first orders for components were issued on 9 January 1973. The steel bodywork, entirely hand made by Ghia in Turin, was delivered in mid-April and the completed concept car was ready to run on 25 May, two weeks before deadline.

'I've spent forty years at Ford', said Piziali, 'but we've never worked so fast, so hard and in such systematic fashion. And by the way, let me say, never have we worked on such an exciting project with so much freedom. It's not every day that you get the chance to create the best car possible, starting with a blank sheet of paper.'

It was a period of feverish and exciting activity for the cost analysts and accountants too. Schimmel's staff had spent hours comparing their figures with those of the experimental engineers, trading an extra expense of a few cents on one piece

A Ghia production, this station-wagon version of the Wolf prototype was developed by Tom Tjaarda at the beginning of 1973.

The Wolf in its 'coupé-sedan' version. This styling project was to have a major influence on the final Bobcat prototype design.

for a new cut in the cost of another. Thirty German cost analysts had been temporarily transferred from Merkenich to Dearborn to set Schimmel's figures against their own which were based on European conditions. The calculations, which had been theoretical at first, were adapted to take account of European rates of pay, fringe benefits, social security charges and current rates of production. It was also Europe which had to supply the essential technical data and detailed figures regarding the transmission unit as the Americans lacked experience with front-wheel drive.

By June the 'Red Book' of the Bobcat had taken shape. At Ford, the Red Book is the bible for every new model. It is a monumental work, weighing several pounds. It has nothing in common with the same colour booklet which guides the thoughts of contemporary China, but looks like a mere pamphlet in comparison. Ford's Red Book is a vehicle set out in detail down to the last nut and bolt, with the price, the description, the dimensions, the weight and the production methods to be employed to make each component, along with the many and various standards to be complied with by those who supply it.

The chief characteristic of this particular Red Book was that although compiled in Detroit, it was expressed in European terms. At every stage account had been taken of European structures, of the technical organisation and production methods used in Europe. The 1972 Escort as produced in Germany had served as a basis. Definitions, methods and systems were carefully translated into European jargon so that the book could immediately be utilised as a working guide at Merkenich or Dunton, just as well as if it had been compiled on the spot.

'We mustn't ask Europe to adapt to us,' said Bob Blank, the co-ordinator of the project, 'we must adapt ourselves to Europe, right from the beginning.'

In this respect Bobcat marked Ford's first steps towards the integration of their methods and systems on a worldwide scale just five years after the campaign for integration in Europe had begun.

These 'B-car' mock-ups produced in Dearborn were still a long way from the final compact shape of Bobcat.

Dearborn's 'concept car' was photographed against the background of a typical American model before being handed over to European designers and engineers.

Sperlich produced the final report on these nine months of gestation like a victory bulletin. The final estimates showed that the direct production cost of Bobcat, in equal economic conditions, would be precisely 100 dollars and 36 cents less than that of the Escort, i.e. some 11 per cent cheaper. Bobcat would weigh 1,574lb or 713.688 kg, that is 245lb less than the Escort used for comparison. The Fiat 127 weighed 706 kg, the Renault 5L 730 kg. The number of separate parts necessary to make a Bobcat would be 2,943 for a two-door model without lift-up rear door, against 4,077 for an equivalent Escort.

The savings achieved had never been bought at the expense of the intrinsic quality of the pre-prototype. But two parts and one dollar had been saved by replacing the Escort steering wheel with a simpler type already proven on the Pinto. One part and nearly two dollars had been saved by adopting a Fiat-style road wheel without nave plate. The Bobcat engine, though for the time being similar to that used in the Escort, needed thirty fewer parts, 506 against 536. Another 36 were saved on the steering column and wheel by adopting a new system of construction and a simplified method of fabrication. As to weight saving, they had gone as far as possible in making systematic use of the old 'offall' method, to use an expression borrowed from the butchers. Etymologically it is derived from 'off-all', the action of the butcher as he cuts away from the meat everything which could be prejudicial to its quality: fat, skin and bones. The Bobcat engineers had also cut things to the bone, not only to bring down the weight but also to avoid all unnecessary waste. During the pressing operations they would cut off a superfluous piece of metal here, while at the same time shaping it so that it could be used somewhere else. No waste, no excess fat, and whenever possible, two parts rather than one from any single movement of the presses.

*

Henry Ford and Lee Iacocca were among the first to drive Bobcat on the secret test track at Dearborn. Henry Ford drives hard, but Iacocca is not to be outdone in any way. All

From Mini-Mite to Bobcat, here are some of the many ways of designing a small car's front.

Variations on a theme. Competition was fierce between designers at Dunton, Merkenich, Turin and Dearborn to develop as 'universal' a body as possible for Bobcat.

the competing cars had been lined up for them. They passed from the Fiat to the Bobcat, from Bobcat to Renault and from Renault to Honda, coming back finally to Bobcat.

'Good package!' said Henry Ford.

Bobcat was still only a full-sized working model, but it already contained the ingredients of success. It was now up to Europe to go to work on this bundle of ideas and Europe was ready to take over. While Detroit had been working on Bobcat, Merkenich and Dunton had been getting the Brenda prototype ready. It had monopolised all their energies for a year, but the staff were now ready to take on a new project.

Phil Caldwell, chairman of Ford-Europe was about to leave London for Detroit where he was to supervise the whole of Ford's international operations. Bill Bourke was to succeed him.

'Send us Bobcat. We're ready,' he said to Henry Ford.

The European management was already familiar with the project down to the smallest details. Better still, they had closely collaborated on it at various levels. In fact this had been going on from the beginning of the year at the express wish of Henry Ford.

'We must associate Europe with this project right away and not just impose it upon them from outside when it is ready.'

In Turin, obviously, Tom Tjaarda at Ghia-de Tomaso and Filippo Sapino as head of the Ford studios had taken part in the design studies for the bodywork right from the beginning. The final project bore their trademark. But the other design teams at Merkenich and Dunton led by Uwe Bahnsen and Jack Telnack had not been idle either.

Taking the Wolf as a starting point, Bahnsen and Telnack combined it with the new Ford family theme expressed in the Capri II and the new Escort, to produce some two-dimensional mock-ups which were to be shown to the European and American managements in June. The technique they employed was a new one. First the outline of the car is drawn full size on a board, then all the metal parts are cut out in plywood which is coloured, lacquered and fixed to the board. The illusion of a three-dimensional model is completed by adding real glass for the windows and two real wheels and tyres. It is quick, economical and above all expressive. It enabled the European designers to meet the 21 June 1973 deadline to put forward their ideas against those already introduced in the Bobcat pre-prototype.

While following Dearborn's endeavours with interest sometimes tinged with scepticism, the European executives had always been inwardly convinced that they could do still better than Sperlich's boys. But come what may, they never doubted that Bobcat was an absolute necessity for them and for the future of Ford-Europe.

The need had been amply confirmed by the second wave of market research undertaken in Europe. While the clinics at Lausanne, San Mateo and São Paulo had allowed designers and engineers to move ahead, they had left too many fundamental questions unanswered for the taste of top management.

So immediately on returning from their Brazilian outing, John Tighe's team had taken to the road again in Europe. Between January and April 1973 an investigation was launched in five European countries to assess the commercial prospects of Bobcat as precisely as possible: total potential sales volume, possible percentage of 'conquest' sales to be added to the total already achieved by Ford, and potential increase in Escort sales due to owners of Bobcat moving up the range.

The investigation was conducted in two stages. First, seven thousand potential buyers of small cars were interviewed in their homes in Great Britain, Germany, France, Italy and Spain. These interviews led to a number of conclusions, some of which were unexpected.

It appeared first of all that Bobcat would only detract very slightly from the sales of Brenda, the new Escort for 1975. In all the countries concerned, Bobcat would considerably increase Ford's market penetration but not in the way the market analysts had previously expected. They had estimated that with Ford then selling about 300,000 Escorts a year in the five countries under consideration, the arrival of Bobcat would reduce these sales to 194,000 units a year. As the sales of Bobcat were expected to stabilise at 281,000 units a year, Ford would have a combined sale of 475,000 Escorts and Bobcats.

The market picture emerging from the interviews completely overturned these forecasts. It now appeared that the arrival of Bobcat would not reduce the sales of the Escort by more than 25,000 a year. On the other hand, total sales of Bobcat itself might not exceed 220,000 units, giving a combined total of 495,000 cars a year. This conclusion in no way reduced the importance of launching Bobcat. On the contrary, other investigations had shown that the car had a potential annual sale of 138,000 in the United States, 80,000 to 100,000 in Brazil, and 19,000 in Argentina, so there would be no problem in disposing of them. What was encouraging, on the other hand, and very important for those who would eventually have to give Bobcat the green light, was that the programme would have no lasting harmful effect on the sales of the Escort.

Previous estimates compiled on a theoretical basis showed that the loss of Escort sales due to the arrival of Bobcat (forecast as 107,000 units per annum) could never be completely compensated for by Bobcat buyers trading up to Escorts. The conclusions of this latest market research were infinitely more optimistic. As the Escort was not expected to lose more than 25,000 yearly sales in the markets under review, this model would regain its previous level of sales only six years after the launch of Bobcat and increase them appreciably from then on.

The inquiry provided other useful information. It thus appeared that 71 per cent of those interviewed would prefer a model with three doors, regardless of price, and that such a model would increase Bobcat sales 35 per cent above forecast.

Moreover it was shown that although very well known (only Fiat and Renault came out better in this respect), Ford did not have the best of all images. In the order of 'favourable opinions' BMW was placed first by the B-Car owners, followed by Peugeot, Fiat, Volkswagen, Citroen, Renault, British Leyland, and then Ford.

Only 8 per cent in Great Britain, 5 per cent in Germany, 9 per cent in France, 6 per cent in Italy and 19 per cent in Spain nominated Ford as their favourite make. Ford gained points everywhere for styling but lost them under the heading of technical sophistication.

Hundreds of sketches were required to progressively develop Bobcat's final profile.

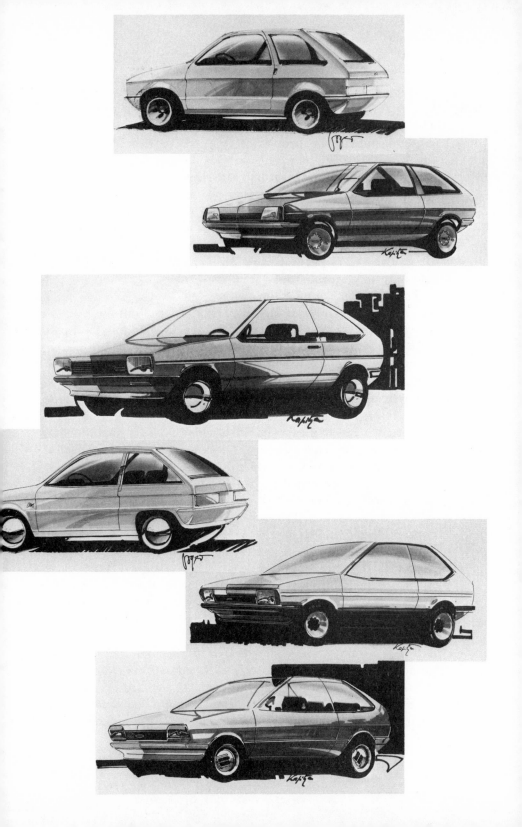

These negative opinions were due in large measure to the fact that Ford was not represented in the small car market. This emerged clearly from another conclusion produced by the inquiry; among the people interviewed, between 58 per cent (in Italy) and 86 per cent (in Spain) would willingly have bought a B-Class Ford if it had appeared 'suitable'.

The inquiry also revealed that the image of the country of origin can influence buying decisions. 90 per cent of the people interviewed preferred a car built in Germany, 83 per cent would have chosen one coming from France, 79 per cent from Great Britain, 77 per cent from Sweden, 76 per cent from Italy and only 45 per cent from Spain.

The investigation also yielded a profile of the average small car buyer: 27 per cent are women, 34 per cent are single; average age is 38 and average income 5,000 dollars, Spain influencing the figures downwards in each case. It is interesting to note that small cars in the Bobcat class cover a greater average distance per annum than class C vehicles: 10,600 miles per year against 9,600, something which would be taken into account when establishing the durability criteria for Bobcat. It is moreover mechanical reliability which is the primary factor influencing purchasing decisions, taking precedence over road holding, fuel economy and the initial purchase price.

The studies confirmed the essential nature of certain techni-cal features: 54 per cent of those questioned favoured front-wheel drive (against 20 per cent for rear-wheel drive); 50 per cent preferred independent rear suspension and only 13 per cent opted for a rigid rear axle; finally, 62 per cent favoured disc brakes against 14 per cent who remained faithful to drums. In conclusion, the inquiry revealed that these owners of class B Cars would choose engines with a cylinder capacity between 760 and 1,150 cc. With its 957 cc that of the base Bobcat was a happy medium.

These results were confirmed in the course of five more clinics organised in early spring in London, Düsseldorf, Paris, Milan and Madrid. The experimental De Tomaso car was this time opposed by Cheetah, the prototype of a shortened Escort with rear-wheel drive. The front-wheel drive car pulverised its opponent. The die was well cast: if Bobcat was to emerge one day, it must be as an entirely new and modern front-wheel drive car, capable of fully satisfying the needs and desires expressed by the market.

*

On 15 June 1973 at 20 h 50, the concept car built in Detroit, landed at Frankfurt in the hold of a cargo plane. A packing case protected it from inquisitive eyes. Two days later, in the Design Centre at Merkenich, the case was opened and Bobcat was unpacked in the utmost secrecy.

It was now Europe's turn.

The 'Cheetah', a shortened Ford
Escort prototype, was voted down
by a sample of potential buyers.

'THE PEOPLE SAY YES!'

Letters and postcards by the sackful were piling up in Henry Ford's outer office at Dearborn. Some had come direct, some via the United States embassy in Madrid, according to whether they had been addressed to 'Mr Ford, Dearborn U.S.A.' or simply 'Mr Ford, U.S.A.'

By the beginning of 1973 everyone in Spain knew that Ford was thinking of building a factory there. They also knew that it would be a bonanza for the town that was chosen. At Talavera de la Reina, near Toledo, they didn't waste any time. Justiniano Luengo, the mayor, launched a public appeal to the townspeople, mobilised the inhabitants of the surrounding villages, and set everyone, children, grown-ups, old people, to work on his plan.

'Everyone, but everyone, must write to Mr Ford and ask him to build his factory at Talavera.'

The town council nominated an official, Melio Casa Rubio, to run the campaign. Soon nearly 75,000 cards and letters arrived at Dearborn. It was an impressive demonstration even if a few correspondents had been so carried away by enthusiasm that they had written several times.

'Come to us, Mr Ford.'

'We want you!'

'Talavera needs you!'

'You make cars all over the world, Mr Ford, but we promise you that here at Talavera we'll make the best and most beautiful of all!'

Henry Ford was touched.

'We must reply individually to everyone,' he said.

He dictated and signed a letter. A specialist organisation, Address Iberica, was mobilised to decipher all the signatures and verify the addresses. It was decided that all the replies

must arrive on the same day. Brought in bulk to the Talavera post office on 29 January 1973, they were all delivered on 30 January. Instead of a factory, every inhabitant of Talavera de la Reina now has a facsimile signature from Henry Ford. It cost a small matter of ten thousand dollars to answer everyone.

Nobody wrote from Valencia or from Almusafes. Nevertheless that was where the plant was to be built. The final decision was taken on 14 June 1973 and the next day Dick Holmes submitted his resignation. To Bill Bourke who was then president of Ford-Europe and who was to become its chairman a fortnight later, he explained.

'I've been happy at Ford, But you'll never find me another job as exciting as this one has been. I've fixed things in Spain that a lot of people thought were impossible. I'm a promoter, not a factory manager. What can I look forward to now?'

'You've really thought this over, Dick?'

'Sure.'

'Well, we will miss you. Thank you for everything you've done.'

Holmes left and went on to set up and run the subsidiary of an American equipment manufacturer, opening Europe up for them. All the same, Ford could have used him to deal with a lot of the unsolved problems that still remained at Valencia and Madrid.

Ford-España, the group's Spanish subsidiary, was officially created on 26 September 1973. The man appointed to run it had wide experience. Carl Levy, 48, had been directing Ford-France after a spell as head of Ford-Norway. He knew everything about selling cars and that's just what he needed, because one of his assignments would be to create a sales network in Spain starting from nothing. But he was also experienced at negotiating with public authorities, since he had conducted the talks which had led to the creation of a model

75,000 postcards and letters were sent from Talavera de la Reina to convince Henry Ford to establish the Spanish factory there. Justiniano Luengo, the mayor (right), and Melio Casa Rubio (left) organized this unsuccessful drive.

113

automatic transmissions plant at Blanquefort, near Bordeaux.

When Levy arrived in Madrid, he alone was the whole Ford Motor Company. The first and only employee of Ford-España, he started working out of his hotel room. It took time before he could set up a tiny office in the Eurobuilding hotel. He did not even have a car. His wife Helen had to drive down in her French-registered Escort to act as Ford-España's first chauffeur. She went around buying the first pencils, paper clips, notebooks and waste paper baskets for the company.

When the first of the staff arrived from Warley and Cologne, they camped out in three rooms while waiting to settle in to their offices on the eighth floor of a newly completed building on the prestigious Avenida Generalissimo.

The first Spaniard to be taken on by Levy was a plump little character, cheerful, lively and astute, who had been recommended by Antonio Garrigues. He knew everyone in Madrid, and everyone knew him. His name was Abilio Bernaldo de Quiros. He had been a journalist, a top government official and director of the Spanish tourist bureau. He was made director of public affairs for the new company and quickly directed himself down to Almusafes; there were enough problems there to keep him busy for some time.

The land on which the Ford factory was to be built belonged to no fewer than 636 different owners. The state had authorised compulsory purchase of the whole site, but for Ford there was no question of driving people off their land against their will. You do not start making business in a new area by antagonising all the local population. Experts had been engaged to fix a fair price for the land. The traditional unit of measure in the province of Valencia is the hanegada, which is 831 square meters or 8,945 square feet. Ford offered the top price: 80,000 pesetas per hanegada. The owners were tempted to sell. When the first of them, a farmer by the name of Jose Melia Company, agreed to part with his plot of sixteen hanegadas, praise was heaped upon him by the whole Spanish press, but by November 1973, the agreements to sell land at Almusafes accounted for no more than 14 per cent of the total factory area.

114

What had happened was that a committee of landowners had been formed. The people running it were some of the wealthiest farmers in the area. They had land elsewhere. Without admitting it publicly, they were afraid that the arrival of Ford, with the industrial wages that the company could pay, would force up agricultural wages. They further feared that a lot of farm hands would prefer to change their jobs altogether and work for Ford. So the committee put pressure on the other landowners to refuse to sell their plots.

'Just wait' said the leaders of the committee. 'Wait, there's no hurry.'

So they waited. But Ford were getting impatient. They did not want to push anyone around, but time was running out and if necessary Ford would have to go somewhere else.

Abilio de Quiros went down from Madrid to make it clear to the mayor.

'If your fellow citizens don't want to do business with us, we won't force their hands.'

Jose Melia Company (left) was first to sell his land at Almusafes to Ford. Carl Levy, president of Ford Spain, publicly handed his cheque over to him.

'But we want Ford!' said Vicente Bosch. 'We want your factory right here.'

Oranges were not selling well and the mayor dreamed of a modern, dynamic prosperous Almusafes. He was a man of the land; all his life he had hardly ever travelled beyond the boundaries of the province. But his son had been to university. He had left with a diploma in engineering and was working in London. Vicente Bosch wanted Ford in Almusafes. Ford, to him, was the key to a brighter future for his people.

He and De Quiros were sitting drinking a bottle of red wine, that rich, heavy *vino tinto* of Spain.

'What can we do?' the mayor asked.

'Get all the landowners together and explain the situation to them,' suggested Ford's man. 'If half the owners agree to sell us their land, we'll stay and we'll put compulsory purchase orders on the rest. But if we have a majority against us, we'll just give up and go somewhere else. I'll give you one week. Let's see how it goes then.'

'Agreed,' said the mayor, and he raised his glass to the success of his mission and the future of the Ford plant.

*

The news spread like wildfire. The press checked it, then ran the story. Spontaneously the youngsters of Almusafes, then of the whole region, gathered in the village square. Banners started appearing.

'Youth wants Ford!' 'Ford for Almusafes!' 'Long live Ford!'

Soon Valencia and the whole province were involved.

An inhabitant of Almusafes who had taken his children to Valencia to buy them some shoes was questioned by the sales girl.

'Are you from Almusafes?'

'Yes, I come from Almusafes!'

'Right. Well I'm sorry, we don't sell shoes to people from Almusafes. By turning down Ford you are turning down the future of the whole region.'

116

Long ago when the railway had come their way, Almusafes had refused to have a train station, so one was built instead at Benifayo, a few miles further on.

'Now we have to walk all the way to Benifayo to catch a train,' the young people complained. 'And look what's happened. Benifayo has become a small town and Almusafes is still just a big village. Surely you're not going to do the same thing with Ford?'

'If you don't sign, I'll leave home,' said one son to his father.

The following Thursday, at 6 pm, Abilio Bernaldo de Quiros returned to Almusafes. Three thousand people were assembled in the square in front of the village hall, holding up banners and posters.

'So, what's the percentage now, Mr Mayor?' de Quiros asked.

'Ninety-six per cent of the landowners have signed their agreements to sell!' said Vicente Bosch.

A broad smile lit up the mayor's long gaunt face.

'What is your decision?' he asked.

'We stay, Mr Mayor. Ford will come to Almusafes. Let's drink to our future.'

'Wait,' said the mayor. 'We must tell them first.'

Posters in front of the town hall at Almusafes: 'Youth says *yes* to Ford!'

117

The two men stepped on to the balcony and looked down on the crowd.

'I have some news for you,' said the mayor. 'Good news. Ford is coming to Almusafes.'

Bosch hugged Ford's envoy. The crowd went wild with joy. They jumped, they danced, they embraced each other. The party went on late that night.

Next day, the papers in Valencia and Madrid carried big headlines: 'The people say Yes to Ford!'

Some 625 owners sold their land to Ford voluntarily at prices varying between 90,000 and 125,000 pesetas. Only eleven had to be expropriated.

Over at headquarters, Ford immediately decided that the future Spanish factory should start production in August 1976 with a single model: the Escort. A year later, in August 1977, the Taunus would join it on the Almusafes assembly lines.

But these plans were soon to be upset by two events. One was the fact that the Bobcat project reached maturity. And then, a few months later, there was the Yom Kippur war which plunged the industrial world into a turmoil the like of which it had never known before: the energy crisis.

*

On 19 June 1973, Henry Ford and all his top management were at Bordeaux for the inauguration of the new Blanquefort factory. It was there, among some of the most renowned vineyards in the world, that Ford had built his European plant for automatic transmissions, most of which in the beginning were to be exported to the United States.

Henry and Cristina Ford were guests of the Baron Elie de Rothschild. The previous evening they had enjoyed a collector's item together: a Chateau-Lafite 1890! Accompanied by his friend Pierre Tari, owner of the Chateau-Giscours, Henry Ford had met many of the proprietors of the great vineyards to reassure them that Ford was not going to pollute the area. Every precaution had been taken to make sure that the wine growing would not suffer in any way from the arrival of industry.

The factory was officially inaugurated by Jacques Chaban-Delmas, mayor of Bordeaux and a former Prime Minister. Henry Ford left for Cologne the same evening, but before taking off, he took good care to check that the two cases of Chateau-Lafite which had been presented to him were safely loaded aboard his private jet.

The Bobcat prototype had arrived at Merkenich five days before the top management, escorted by two of its fathers, Erik Reickert and Bob Torkelson who had been transfered to Europe along with the car. For another two months, Reickert was to continue commuting between Detroit and Europe to ensure a smooth transfer of the project. The pre-prototype was now officially handed over to the European technicians and the Americans who had conceived it would have no further part in its existence except to put up a last fight for their ideas on styling. But in fact their design project was eventually to be rejected in favour of one evolved at Merkenich and Dunton.

The product planning committee met at Merkenich on 21 June with Henry Ford in the chair. It was not their job to ratify the project; only the board of directors could do that and it was agreed that the board's approval would be requested at its December meeting. But it was decided to move the project from the 'advanced pre-programme' status to that of a 'pre-programme'. This did not amount to a definite commitment, but was a sure sign that Bobcat was now moving.

Among the technical decisions, it was laid down that the Kent engine used in the Escort should serve as the basis of a modernised engine for the Bobcat. As for styling, it was confirmed that the Wolf prototype evolved by Ghia should serve as the basic theme for the side view and especially for the large window areas that were to figure on the definitive prototype, but that the front and rear lines should develop the concepts sketched in Bahnsen's two-dimensional design. Finally, the committee gave the management of Ford-Europe full authority to set up the best qualified team possible to work on it.

It meant a new approach on all fronts. Bit by bit new organisations were created, unprecedented methods of control and co-ordination were worked out and a real team of 'Incor-

119

ruptibles' was mobilised under Reickert's direction to push forward a programme which was already turning out to be the most ambitious and the most difficult in the history of Ford, and perhaps in the history of the whole motor industry. It was an automobile man's nightmare: making an entirely new product using techniques completely different from the ones with which the corporation is familiar; a car which would apparently have to be build in a new country—Spain—in a new factory and with inexperienced workers. Its mechanical parts were to come from a great variety of different sources; a network of suppliers had to be created from scratch; and finally it was a European car which would have to establish itself as a universal vehicle to be sold, and perhaps even made, on a worldwide basis; in Europe, naturally, but in the United States too, and in Brazil for South America, and in Australia for Asia and the Pacific region.

But they had not got that far yet. The first task was to set up the working parties and push ahead with the analysis of the project. It was Erik Reickert's job to transfer all the responsibility and all the archives from Detroit to Dunton and Merkenich. He took just long enough to telephone his wife.

'We're settling in Europe, dear, sell the house and come on over!'

He had to start from scratch and set up a new planning team. He took quarters in any place he could find, with Torkelson and a secretary. Ford allocated him an old conference room at the HQ at Warley. Out of *Warley* and the conference *room* he made his 'War room', an operational base as simple and stark as a military one, where he worked fourteen hours a day to compile minutely the technical and financial report which was to give birth to the Bobcat. He ate in the office and sometimes slept there. The chairs were covered with lunch boxes which his secretary brought from the canteen.

One day when Hans Schaberger, president of Ford-Germany had come to see him and was told to take a seat, the visitor looked round at the chairs all loaded with food boxes.

'There aren't any seats. Nothing but grub.'

'Right. Then have something to eat.'

120

The two-dimensional renderings of Bobcat which were presented by Ford Europe designers on 21 June 1973. They moved away from the pre-prototype. Bobcat-Fiesta was around the corner.

To build up his team, Reickert enrolled everyone available on the spot, then called Detroit for reinforcements. America began by sending him six production engineers. Then came one of the champions of the team, Lou Veraldi, square shouldered, big and solid as a rugby forward. His parents had been born in Calabria, but he had never set foot there himself. Veraldi had started at Ford at the age of 19 as a humble filing clerk in the offices of the chief engineer. Twenty-five years later, now with a diploma in engineering, he was responsible for the whole of the car manufacturing operations at Detroit and he was on the point of launching the Mustang II. It was just a few days before the assembly lines were due to start moving and the atmosphere in the Dearborn plant was highly charged, when Veraldi was told he was wanted on the phone by World Headquarters.

'The hell with it. I've no time,' said he.

At the third call, he sent someone to say he was not there. At the fourth he finally went to the phone.

'Phil Caldwell here,' said the voice.

'Hello, Mr Caldwell,' replied Veraldi.

Caldwell, the chairman of Ford-Europe up to then, was now an executive vice-president of the corporation, in charge of all its international activities.

'I need you for Europe,' he said.

'I'm busy. I've got to launch the Mustang...'

'I know, Lou.'

'When do I leave?'

'Finish the Mustang launch and then take a few days vacation. We'll expect you in London by the end of September.'

*

At Merkenich the European technicians got hold of the 'concept car'. They found some good points in it but as they got to know this foreign child they were fairly free with their criticisms. The general comfort and road holding seemed competitive with those of the Fiat 127 which was still the basis of

122

Lew Veraldi: from Mustang II to Bobcat.

comparison, but they thought the driving position was poor, the steering column vibrated excessively, the gear shift was not yet precise enough and they found the suspension too soft. They also had doubts about the dependability of the revolutionary front suspension and about the possibility of mass producing a torsion bar like the one which had been devised in Detroit. Such reservations were only natural at this stage and they didn't worry Bill Bourke, newly installed at the helm of Ford-Europe.

'They've provided us with a concept. It's up to us to turn it into a car,' he said.

What mattered was that the fundamental data in the 'Red Book' seemed acceptable to the European cost analysts and engineers within a dollar or two. The main points were drawn up as usual in two opposite columns headed 'Risks' and 'Opportunites'. The two columns roughly balanced out.

Beyond these reservations about details, a whole series of major strategic decisions remained to be settled, beginning with the choice of the factory where the new car would eventually be built. Obviously it would be tempting to turn over the future Spanish plant to Bobcat.

Iacocca said: 'We had planned to produce Escorts and then the Taunus at Valencia. If we have to get a set of new presses and new tooling for Spain we might just as well start from scratch and equip the plant with what it needs to produce an entirely new car.'

Everyone agreed in principle, but it was easier said than done. The production programme had already been approved by the Spanish authorities and the replacement of a conventional car like the Escort, which could have used engines and transmissions imported from England and Germany, with a front-wheel drive model like Bobcat raised the problem of where the engines and transmissions were to be made.

For a long time Henry Ford and Giovanni Agnelli, the head of Fiat, had thought about the possibility of cooperation between their companies. The previous year, Giovanni's brother Umberto Agnelli had been to Detroit, where he and Henry Ford had looked at various projects which the two corporations might be able to carry out together. During the initial phases of the Bobcat project, Ford had examined the possibility of buying engines and even front-drive transmissions from Honda to equip the future small car, but the idea had been dropped. Then Oscar Montabone, Fiat's chief engineer, visited the team engaged on the Bobcat project in Detroit. The idea that emerged was that Ford might collaborate with SEAT, Fiat's associates in Spain, to create a joint factory to produce front-drive transmissions.

Henry Ford and Giovanni Agnelli talked about it on the telephone.

'It looks interesting to me,' said Ford. 'Let's get our engineers to look it over. It they think it's a technically sound

Before freezing the final prototype, shapes were refined on one-dimensional drawings and scaled-down mock-ups. The birth of a car is a matter of time and patience.

Wood frames and plasticine are being used to make the full scale mock-up, which will serve to judge the final lines of the car and start wind-tunnel tests. Similar care is taken to define interior decoration for the prototype.

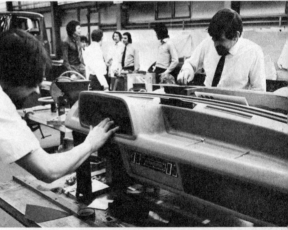

The car is taking shape, but it still is no more than a mock-up without chassis nor mechanical components. Shapes and measurements provided by this mock-up will help build the first mechanical prototype, ready for actual driving.

proposition, we can meet to set it up. It could be a good chance to get something going together.'

'I absolutely agree,' said Agnelli.

The creation of a common factory by the two groups could have reduced the total investment needed from Ford. Moreover, Fiat had a rich and ancient experience in front-wheel drive.

'That experience could be useful to us,' said Henry Ford to his people. 'We always try to do too much by ourselves. Let's see what we and SEAT can do together.'

Talks began on two planes, industrial and technical. Despite Henry Ford's obvious desire to reach an agreement to cooperate, his specialists approached the affair with the greatest prudence. Quite soon, unfavourable reports began accumulating on Henry Ford's desk.

'We won't save much by working with them,' repeated Bill Hayden, the man in charge of manufacturing.

'Well, try just the same,' he replied.

Then the technicians added their verdict.

'Their transmission is already old and it's not as good as all that. It would be hard to guarantee quality up to our standards.'

Little by little it emerged that Fiat would not be able to supervise their end of the operation closely enough to suit Ford. In effect SEAT would be the principals in the deal and the Spanish company, jealous of its independence, would not let Fiat have much say in the matter. A cable went to Henry Ford:

'If Fiat is not directly involved we can't commit ourselves to this deal.'

At Merkenich there were still some engineers who had experience of front-wheel drive. They had learned their lessons the hard way with the front-drive Taunus which had been developed from the Detroit-designed Cardinal some years previously. Proud of their current gearboxes, which are among the world's best, they went all out to create their own front-drive transmission repeating to anyone who would listen:

'We can do better than Fiat and we must remain independent of SEAT.'

129

Finally, it was Lou Veraldi who convinced Henry Ford.

'We've done a lot of work and we're certain we can do a better job than Fiat.'

'For how much?'

'It won't cost any more than going to SEAT. We might even gain a bit in all departments: weight, cost and quality.'

'Who will do it?'

'Jo Renierkeens, in Germany.'

'Jo? He's the one who did the box for the Pinto. He's really tops in this game, isn't he? If he does it I believe you are right, we will have a better transmission...'

Bill Bourke supported Veraldi.

'We haven't got sufficient guarantees of support from Fiat at the production level. It will be difficult for engineers from Turin to intervene in the SEAT plant. We can't take the risk of being dependent on someone else for such an important item.'

'I suppose you're right,' said Henry Ford.

'The only snag is that this makes things more complicated,' said Bourke. 'Up to now we've had one programme, the Bobcat. Now we have two, Bobcat and the new transmission!'

If Ford was to go it alone in producing the new transmission, they would need a new factory to make it. Where would they put it?

*

When Ford had decided to erect a plant at Bordeaux to build automatic transmissions, Henry Ford had promised Georges Pompidou, then Prime Minister of France, that his next European assembly plant would be built in his country. For obvious strategic reasons, he had been forced to choose Spain instead, but he wanted to redeem his promise to Pompidou, in part at least. Meanwhile the latter had succeeded General de Gaulle as President of the Republic.

Henry Ford went to visit him at the Elysee Palace before the end of the year. Bill Bourke was with him, and Vic Dial,

130

president of Ford-France, who acted as interpreter. Pompidou had only four months to live and he had put on a lot of weight under the influence of the cortisone injections he was receiving, but Henry Ford found him in very good form.

'Our Bordeaux plant is a great success,' he said. 'The building operations went very smoothly. In fact the techniques we used to construct it and get it into operation have now become standard practice in our organisation.'

'I'm delighted,' said Pompidou.

'We'd like to double the size of the plant, Monsieur le President, so that we can build transmissions at Bordeaux for a completely new car. For us it's a logical decision. The products have a lot in common and we can use the same technical staff to supervise the production.'

Pompidou smiled.

'I would have preferred a complete car assembly plant!'

'We can't do it yet. Not this time,' said Ford. 'But I hope it will come.'

'I hope so too, Mr Ford, and I wish you luck with this project.'

Pompidou accompanied his guests out to the palace portico, walking slowly, but without apparent difficulty. That concluded the affairs of State. Before returning to the Plaza-Athenée, his usual hotel in Paris, Henry Ford had one more call to make in the Faubourg Saint-Honore. This one was almost as important! The latest Paris gown bought by his wife Cristina had needed a few alterations. Henry Ford collected the garment on his way, to deliver it in Detroit the next day.

Cristina Ford would be happy. She wanted to wear that gown at Christmas!

Lee Iacocca and the Bobcat prototype at Cologne on 2 October 1973, 1049 days before planned production start.

ONE THOUSAND DAYS TO GO

Erik Reickert was back in Detroit. He was still commuting between Europe and America and he kept an office in Ford's World Headquarters. The telephone rang. Ford-Europe on the line.

'Erik, will you do something for us?' the voice said.

'Sure. What is it?'

'We want to make a parting presentation to Phil Caldwell and we thought of the stuffed head of a bobcat, but we can't find one in London.'

'You're crazy! I've got better things to do than go hunting dead cats.'

'Look, Erik, the guys are set on it.'

'Alright, alright. I'll see. How much do you want to spend?'

'I don't know what they cost. Two hundred dollars maybe?'

Eventually Reickert found the animal in a naturalist's shop in a Detroit suburb; about two feet long, with narrow shoulders and big paws. The head was very fine, with scarcely a whisker missing. Reickert called London on the direct line which connects all Ford's national headquarters.

'I've found what you want. It only costs a hundred dollars. It's beautifully stuffed. But it's a whole bobcat.'

'Then get him to cut the head off. We only want the head to put it on a plaque.'

'You'll take the lot, or you'll get nothing.'

Reickert had the stuffed bobcat photographed and had a giant colour print made of it. In London, they gave Phil Caldwell this poster-sized picture at a farewell dinner and when he arrived in Detroit he found the stuffed bobcat already installed in his office on the twelfth floor.

But Reickert had a further use for the lynx's picture. He got a local craftsman to make an engraving from it and then produce some small bronze badges of the Bobcat head. It could be used both as a tiepin or as a lapel badge.

On 2 October 1973, in Cologne, 150 Ford staff were thus initiated into the Order of the Bobcat. They formed the basic team responsible for the future small car. The badge marked them out as men with a special mission.

They did not yet know just how much it was going to demand of them in sustained and concentrated effort. They had come together from all over Europe, from Detroit, from Australia and Latin America. Some of them were on the permanent staff of Ford-Europe, but there was also a whole battalion of 'Foreign Service Employees'. These are the globe trotters of the International Division who rarely spend more than five years in any one job. Through force of circumstance they learn to make themselves understood in a great variety of tongues, but they really have only one language in common, not so much English as 'Fordese'...

They were gathered together in the ballroom of Cologne's Intercontinental Hotel. On the left of the platform from which Henry Ford and Lee Iacocca were to address the team stood the latest Bobcat prototype. It had been brought from Merkenich in a sealed truck with an escort and installed at the hotel in the utmost secrecy.

Ford greeted them and delivered the opening speech. For many of them it was their first meeting with him. The atmosphere was tense. Henry Ford quickly disposed of the preliminaries. Then Iacocca strode to the the lectern. He was to speak for one hour. It was an oration which will go down in Ford history as the most impassioned appeal ever made to the staff. It was a stirring call to arms. He spoke in short sentences, pungent, direct and precise, full of emphasis and enthusiasm.

'I'm going to pitch you the fastest ball you ever saw in your lives, and none of you better miss it on the rebound. Right, gentlemen, here it is. You have exactly 1,049 days to go. 1,049 days, not one more, may be a few less, before the car you see here has to start rolling off the assembly lines. 1,049 days until the start of production. From now until then, we shall be spending more than 600,000 dollars a day on the Bobcat programme. And I'm not including what we're going to be spending on new factories.

'Someone has pointed out that 1976 is a leap year. That's fine. It means you've got one extra day. Even so it's a serious challenge. The greatest challenge that we at Ford have ever accepted.

'You're going to set up a new plant in Spain, dealing with new suppliers who have an old-world way of doing things; you're going to be working with people who have a profound belief in the magical virtues of *mañana*, meaning tomorrow. You're going to have to set up a dealer network in Spain, starting with nothing. You'll have to launch a new product. Completely new. There'll be nothing in Bobcat that we have in stock right now. ·

'Everything in this car will be new. And Ford has never yet built a "B" car. It's a blank page. And you've got to do the writing.

'I really mean *you*. All of you gathered together here. Because from tomorrow, 3 October, Bobcat is yours; completely yours. That's why I'm here today. To pass the buck to you. The final decision to make Bobcat will be made in two month's time. I am sure that the board will make it. It will be the most costly product programme in all our history, but it will be approved because it is already very late. We may be the last to get into the small car market. That's why we must also be the best.'

In that great ballroom you could have heard a pin drop. They held their breath. Iacocca sketched in the history of the Bobcat project and the hesitations, the doubts and the delays that had preceded it.

'We can't wait any longer, and we can't go back. In Europe alone there will be a market for three million "B" cars by 1980. Perhaps more. Compact, economical cars are now inevitable and from now on their numbers will go on increasing. I firmly believe it and you'd better believe it too.

'And don't forget that we're a worldwide corporation. Ford-Europe by itself would be number 20 among the world's biggest corporations. That's not bad. But people also need small

135

cars in South America, in the Far East, in areas where the automobile markets are at the point where yours were thirty years ago. That's why Bobcat, your car, will be a universal car; a car for the whole world.'

Iacocca predicted a brilliant future for the new model. But he also left them in no doubt about the constraints and disciplines they would have to accept, the amount of work that had to be done, the obstacles to be overcome and targets to be reached. It had to be a thoroughly reliable car, durable, easy to maintain and economical to use but it must also be a refined car, technically and visually, and they must find out how to make it at minimum cost.

He concluded:

'For years people have been talking to me about new ideas, technical revolutions, new concepts, and asking why we stick to conventional cars and traditional designs. Well, here's the new car you wanted. You've got it. Now it's up to you to prove that you can do something new. You have a thousand days to do it. But there are only 240 working days in a year and everyone has a right to vacations. This means each of you has only two years of working time to turn Bobcat into reality. So let's make one firm rule; that no one will ever let twenty-four hours go by before making a decision. That's vital!'

*

Ford and Iacocca set the example. The very next day they presided over the Product Planning Committee at Merkenich. A list of all the major options of the programme was drawn up for submission to the Board meeting which would make the final decisions in December. They also set up some new organisations, in particular a 'Special Products Committee' which would have the job of analysing, coordinating and approving all measures within the merged Bobcat and Eagle programmes. For it was precisely because these two programmes had come together, almost by chance, that Bobcat had become possible.

136

During the same meeting another essential decision was taken. Acceptance of the basic specification of the car, consisting of the twenty 'hard points' which traditionally constitute a sort of technical photo-fit picture of any car. They confirmed that the Bobcat power plant would be derived from the Kent engine, sensibly modified and lightened, and that this engine would not be produced at Dagenham, but more probably in Spain. It was also decided that the final prototype must be completed in another fourteen months, by the beginning of December 1974.

Finally, the committee gave its verdict on the work of the designers and made a number of fundamental choices about the lines of the bodywork. All the styling studies which had been done during the previous months were lined up under the artificial sunlight in the exhibition studio. They came from Dearborn, Turin, Dunton and Merkenich. In all, four mock-ups in clay, and five more in fibre-glass, each one of which had cost about 300,000 dollars!

The choice was quickly narrowed down to two of these studies. One had been produced at Dunton by a team under the leadership of Jack Telnack, former director of design for Ford-Australia. The other was the work of Uwe Bahnsen, a one-time racing driver friend of the late Wolfgang von Trips, and a painter of some distinction, who directs the studios at Merkenich. The two studies were variations on the same theme, established partly by the Ghia's 'Wolf' for the front and rear ends and by a previous study done by the German group for the side view and the general shape of the profile.

The management hesitated between these two projects, which resembled each other quite closely. They found it so difficult to choose between them that for the first time in Ford's history it was agreed to put it to the vote instead of depending on an authoritative choice by the sole top executives. Fifteen men were in attendance who could be divided broadly into three groups: the Americans, with Ford, Iacocca, Caldwell, and Sperlich; the 'European Americans' comprising Bourke, John McDougall, the new president of Ford-Europe, and Jo Oros, the man in charge of design. The third group

137

It was a difficult choice between the Dunton and Merkenich projects. On 3 October 1973, Ford top brass decided in favor of a compromise between these two studies.

These were the major prototypes submitted to Ford's top managment. At this stage of development, the various design projects evolved by the Turin, Dunton, Merkenich

and Dearborn studios had come close to each other. The final version of Bobcat was derived from several of these projects.

consisted of the real Europeans such as Terry Beckett, managing director of Ford-England, and Hans Schaberger, president of Ford-Germany.

Each of them examined the styling prototype minutely, pen and notebook in hand, but even between the three main groups there were differences of opinion. Finally it was the Europeans who swung the balance by eight votes to seven in favour of the Dunton project, but with the proviso that this styling study might be further amended to take account of some ideas which had emerged from Cologne. The general dimensions were still those of the original concept car, the essential guiding principles of which were to be respected right through to the end. Nevertheless Bobcat was already assuming a distincly European character, a character which was to be strengthened continuously throughout every ulterior technical decision made.

Having thus handed over Bobcat officially and set the European machine in motion, Henry Ford and Lee Iacocca climbed once more into the private Gulf Stream II jet which speeds them from one meeting to another. Destination Madrid! The Chairman was to have lunch with members of the Spanish government and would take this opportunity to officially announce the formation of Ford-España SA, while the President went on to Valencia for a quick tour of inspection of the factory site and then took off again for southern Spain, for his next job was to decide on still another factory site, that of the future Bobcat engines plant.

The Spanish government, which wanted to move more industry into the south had offered a location at Algeciras, only a stone's throw from Gibraltar. From the top of the hill which was suggested as a possible site, Iacocca had a magnificent view. On a clear day you could even see Tangiers. But for a factory, Algeciras was at the end of the world. There would be enormous transport problems. Further, the hill would have to be dynamited flat to create a plateau on which the factory could be built.

'Wonderful for vacations!' said Iacocca. 'But as a site for a factory, it's out of the question!'

Provided the Board gave the go-ahead to the whole project, there was only one place to put the engine plant, and that was right alongside the other ones at Valencia. There was space enough there, and plenty of potential labour. Maintenance and transport costs would be cut sharply. Integration of all the industrial resources on one site was the obvious choice. There was now little doubt that the future automotive complex at Valencia would be one of the biggest in the world.

*

Although the company's top brass had decided by then on the general body lines and architecture for the prototype, including interior layout, instrument panel and principal controls, the Bobcat team launched yet another programme of market research. To leave nothing to chance, they had to get a detailed verdict on the acceptability of various features of the existing styling studies. So this time four prototypes were set against the Fiat 127 and the Renault 5 at clinics organised at the Neue Messe in Düsseldorf, the Auberge Chesnay du Roy in the suburbs of Paris, the Exhibition Park in Milan and the Melia Castilla Hotel in Madrid.

The original de Tomaso prototype was wheeled out for its last public appearance alongside the latest American styling study (the thirteenth in a long series) and the three fibreglass cars built at Dunton and Merkenich. The cars from England and Germany established a clear lead over the other Ford studies. Their scores against the Fiat and Renault were appreciably better than anything that had been obtained by the Ghia-de Tomaso prototype during the preceding months.

The 350 potential 'B' car buyers who were invited to pass judgement on the prototypes even preferred these latest Bobcats to the Fiat 127. They gained extra points for interior convenience and visibility, but they were criticised for lack of sufficient space between steering wheel and seat, access to the front seats, headroom in the rear seats and size of the rear luggage compartment.

An additional clinic was organised at Düsseldorf to provide further information on public reaction to some of the details of trim and equipment. Three hundred guinea pigs took part, half of whom were French and Italian selected in Paris and Milan and invited to spend a free day in Germany. They were shown the most perfected Bobcat prototype, but above all they saw five different versions of the instrument panel and five different treatments for the door panels, with and without storage space, with and without armrests.

Finally a separate clinic was organised at the Dunton technical centre with the sole object of evaluating the luggage boot on the scores of space and accessibility.

All these remarks and reactions, criticisms and comparisons were carefully weighed by the designers and engineers when they got down to the job of defining the final prototype. They now had a mass of irrefutable evidence: hundreds of pages stuffed with opinions backed by figures which showed them which way to go.

'A designer can always suggest ideas to the public but it would be crazy not to listen to the answers from the prospective buyers,' says Bahnsen. 'On the whole the public knows better than we do. We must work for them, but also *with* them.'

Ford has come a long way since Henry I, founder of the dynasty, offered potential buyers any colour they liked as long as it was black.

*

Working in close touch with Phil Caldwell in Detroit, Bourke, McDougall, Reickert and their team of experts drew up in London the 'blue letter' on the Bobcat programme. Why 'blue', you may well ask. The simple answer is that the president and the corporate vice presidents traditionally send out their internal memoranda on blue paper. The staff can tell at a glance where such a note comes from and there is less chance of anyone overlooking its importance! More specifically a 'blue letter' is a brief which has the force of law once it has been

As for the body work, a number of variations of the driver's compartment and interior decoration were developed. They were submitted to consumer panels and for final judgment to the 'Product Committee'.

examined and approved by the board. Every new programme has its 'blue letter' which forms the immutable charter that governs its existence. It defines all the essential options as briefly and concisely as possible. It is supplemented by any number of appendices. It has the strength of a constitution, except that it cannot be modified by way of referendum, but only by a decision of the government which adopted it; in this case the supreme Board which meets ten times a year (February and August excepted) at 9.30 a.m. on the second Thursday in the month on the twelfth floor of the Dearborn World HQ.

The way is long and rigorous, which leads a blue letter into the Boardroom. The Yom Kippur war was raging at the eastern end of the Mediterranean, with all its first dire consequences for the economies and energy supplies of the western world when the Product Planning Committee met once more. On 3 December they were at Merkenich and the following day at Dunton. The committee drew up a new series of recommendations for inclusion in the blue letter which was then nearing completion. The final lines of the pre-prototype were officially approved, together with the layout and equipment of the interior. The transmission and final drive were also adopted and the committee confirmed that it would like to have these made at Bordeaux. It also recommended that the engines should be manufactured at Valencia. Finally, it was agreed that the size of the optional engine which would supplement the basic 957 c.c. unit would be reduced from 1,200 to 1,117 c.c.

The draft of the blue letter was then submitted to the various managements for their opinions. There were no special comments from labour relations and design. Marketing and Planning declared themselves in favour but expressed the wish that the programme would not close the door to possible derivatives, an enlarged Bobcat for example which could become a class C car and a 'federalised' Bobcat which could be sold in the United States. The all-powerful financial chiefs considered that the plan involved a certain amount of risk and felt that it could not be justified solely on the basis of expected profits. Nevertheless they gave Bobcat the green light 'in view

146

of the energy crisis'. Finally Environment and Safety declared that they had no objections provided the programme did not turn out to be 'too ambitious'.

On 10 December, Bill Bourke submitted a note ten pages long to the Financial Committee, defending it before a jury as critical as anyone could hope to meet. Three days later, he and Phil Caldwell presented the blue letter to the Board.

They are sixteen, who assemble round a great horseshoe table once a month under the chairmanship of Henry Ford, sixteen who are the council of wise men on whom the fate of

Bill Bourke, chairman of Ford Europe and future head of Ford's North American operations, was to be Bobcat's advocate in front of the Board of Directors. This was the toughest examination for the most expensive project in the company's history.

the company depends. Among them are the chairman's two brothers: Benson who presides over the Dealer Policy Board, the committee which draws up the group policies governing its relationships with the distributors and dealers, and William, vice president in charge of design, who has overall responsibility for the styling studios. With them on the board are the other top officials of the company: Iacocca and the three executive vice-presidents, Bob Hampson who then supervised the whole of the North American activities, Phil Caldwell, responsible for all international operations and Ed Lundy the financial expert.

They are flanked by a string of eminent personalities from outside the organisation: two university chancellors, the publisher of the Times-Mirror newspaper group in Los Angeles, chairmen of other companies like Philip Morris, National Cash Register, Merck & Co., Deltec International, and lastly the president of the Foreign Policy Association, a private group which tries to weigh upon the definition of the U.S. foreign policy. This group is one of the ablest and most influential in the country.

As he was about to step into the boardroom to appear before them for what was to be the last but certainly the most difficult of all the examinations the project had gone through, Bill Bourke adjusted his tie and muttered to himself.

'I must be mad to come and ask them for so much money at this time'.

On that point at least, he found no one to disagree with him!

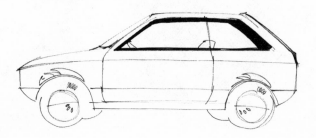

A BLUE LETTER

Bourke went straight into the attack. Before offering them the menu, he presented them with the bill.

'What we are asking for is an additional budget to complete the factory extensions to pay for extra tooling, to launch production and cover the technical costs of the operation.'

While listening to Caldwell and Bourke, the gentlemen of the board nervously fingered through the file which had been handed to them. The blue letter which was itself the most detailed in Ford's history, was backed up by thirty-four appendices and another thirty explanatory documents to justify the hand-out requested by these gamblers from Ford-Europe. They were juggling with millions.

The directors were bombarded with figures. With production in full swing from 1980, they would be making 356,000 Bobcats a year, i.e. 2.9 per cent of total European car production and 12 per cent of all small car output. Sixty per cent of Bobcat sales would be extra sales that Ford could not have made without Bobcat. Ford's total sales in the Common Market, without counting Spain, would thus be increased by 180,000 units a year and Ford's share of European registrations would be raised from 12 to 13.5 per cent. To make it possible, they would be increasing the number of distributors and dealers from 4,200 to 5,800, more than half of this expansion taking place in France, Italy and Spain.

Some of the directors were now adding up the figures. If one put down what had already been spent on Bobcat and added in the credits which had been made available in the previous year for the construction of the Valencia plant, and those which were now being requested to build an additional factory to make the engines in Valencia and a new factory in France for front axles and transmissions, and if one assumed that inflation would inevitably add a few more millions to the estimates, this was a programme which could easily add up to a billion dollars, perhaps more.

'We've never spent so much money at one time', said someone.

Bill Bourke cleared his throat.

'No, sir, we have not.'

'Can we manage it?'

'We have no choice. We've got to do it if Ford is to stay in the running.'

The battle was courteous but tough. It went on for two hours. The smoke of battle was provided by cigars. For refreshment, Henry Ford drank tea as usual; most of the others coffee.

'Nobody has ever made money building Class B cars. What makes you think you can do better than the others?'

'And Spain? Tell me, what's going to happen in Spain? Have you thought about the political situation over there?'

Bourke had an answer for everything. Henry Ford, Iacocca and Caldwell backed him up.

Ten times, using different approaches, Bourke explained that he needed Bobcat if Ford was to survive in Europe, that is to make any progress there. His arguments were detailed and convincing. Class B cars would represent 53 per cent of registrations in Spain, 38 per cent in Italy and 28 per cent in France by the beginning of the eighties. Could they afford to be shut out from such big slices of the market indefinitely?

Admittedly the programme would be a losing proposition between 1974 and 1978, but they would merely be retreating so as to advance more strongly later.

'And don't forget,' Bourke went on, 'that in our calculations we have not taken into account the possibility of building Bobcat in other places besides Europe. America is going to need this car someday.

Henry Ford intervened:

'Just forget that in your present calculations. That's another matter. But it's true there is a good extra potential on this side of the Atlantic.'

150

'Good,' said Bourke. 'Then let me draw your attention to the general effect that Bobcat will have on our overall European operations. A new model always brings a lot of people into the showrooms. Judging by Lincoln-Mercury's experience when they launched the Capri in America, we estimate that the introduction of Bobcat will produce an extra 17,000 sales of other models in the range. Secondly, the enlargement of our dealer network made possible by Bobcat should produce an extra 9,000 sales a year for other models.

'Thirdly, our market research shows that 13 per cent of Bobcat buyers will eventually move up to another Ford model, whereas they would have bought something else if their first car had been another make.

Surrounded by figures, impressed by the clear and detailed analyses which even gave them the projected selling price of the future car, the maintenance cost, the warranty cost and the dealer discounts that would be required, market by market, together with comparative figures for competing models, the members of the board were at last convinced. No formal vote was taken, but in a quick look round the big table, each of the members signified his approval. All the same, a few of them told Bill Bourke:

'You must report progress to us regularly. You should come and see us again at least once every six months.'

'I'll come more often if necessary,' replied the head of Ford-Europe. He did not imagine then, however, that he would have to cross the Atlantic at least once a month during the following year to bring his figures up to date in meetings with the finance men and the top executives at Dearborn.

*

By approving the 'blue letter' on 10 December, 1973, the Board had provided Bobcat with its official birth certificate, and given the send-off to what must be one of the greatest automobile projects in history. And all this was happening in the middle of an energy crisis which had already reduced production to danger point for the automobile industry. At Ford-Germany output and sales dropped like a brick right through 1974, finally coming out 37 per cent below the previous year. Ford-Britain declared a nominal profit:

'Just about enough to pay our telephone and postage bills for the year,' said Terry Beckett, their chairman, with some humour.

In the United States, production bottomed out at 3,090,000 units against 3,400,000 in 1973.

The general economic climate and the state of the car market in particular were not encouraging for a new enterprise on the scale of the Bobcat operation. But in fact it was all the more reason for going flat out to get the show on the road.

Over the years the Ford Motor Company has got the launching of a new model down to a fine art and they have an exact timetable for it. Normally the first examples of a new model roll off the production line 28 months after the programme has been approved by the Board. But on this project the time which had been saved by the work done at Dearborn under Hal Sperlich gave the European technicians some extra margins. It had now been decided that the car was not to be built in Spain exclusively, but also at Saarlouis, the German factory which makes the Escort, and maybe later at the Dagenham plant in England as well. Spain was to be responsible for all the engines (with a maximum potential of 400,000 units a year), France would do all the gearboxes and differentials but body pressings and final assembly would be split between Spain and Germany.

At Valencia they were to produce 254,000 Bobcats a year, to which 110,000 Taunus would be added from 1978 onwards. At Saarlouis the plant was to be enlarged, raising its capacity from 231,000 to 268,000 units a year. At that time they expected a fall in Escort sales (which was later to be proved wrong) and so Saarlouis was credited with a potential of 160,000 rising to 220,000 Bobcats. The decision as to whether Dagenham would be included among the plants assembling Bobcat was put off until later, depending on whether the car was to be sold in the United States also. In the immediate future, Great Britain's contribution would consist of cylinder blocks cast at the Thames foundry, radiators made at Basildon, carburettors and ignition distributors from the Ford plant in Belfast. Production of the complete cars was to start at Saarlouis on 23 August 1976 and at Valencia on 15 November. This time lag would help to ensure that the Spanish cars would have top German quality, as the team responsible for launching production at Saarlouis would then be transferred to Spain to start the Bobcat assembly lines at Valencia-Almusafes.

The European staff thus had 33½ months—five months more than usual—to get Bobcat rolling.

'We will use the time to make the car as perfect as possible, right from the beginning,' Bourke declared. 'But we will try and save some time on this programme if we possibly can.'

Things now started moving swiftly. As Iacocca had said on another occasion, there was not a day to lose.

*

On 19 January 1974, the bulldozers went into action at Valencia. There was only one building, a dilapidated farmhouse, standing on the site at Almusafes. This year no one had planted the usual artichokes and onions; only a few orange trees remained to be flattened.

John McDougall, president of Ford-Europe had come from London with a party of his colleagues to witness the event. He is a small man but a giant in enthusiasm. He is a perfect illustration of success the Ford way. He had been born fifty-seven years earlier of modest Irish family and arrived in Detroit as an immigrant at the age of sixteen. From then on, Ford provided his whole education. He graduated from the Henry Ford Trade School and from Ford's apprentice school. His first job was as a draughtsman at the River Rouge plant in Detroit and he then worked his way patiently through all the ranks in the hierarchy as a manufacturing engineer. From 1971 he had been responsible for all Ford production in Europe and his wide industrial experience made him an ideally qualified president to see through the vast and complex programme from which Bobcat was to emerge.

'I've done a lot of exciting things at Ford,' he said to those who were with him at Almusafes that day, 'but I've never been in charge of anything to compare with this. Just look at those fields. Down there in the middle of those orange groves, we're going to make 400,000 engines a year. Here on this bare hillside we're going to install the press shop. And over there, where you see that old onion field, we shall be assembling nearly 300,000 cars a year. Fantastic! Fantastic!'

At 8.30 a.m. every Monday from then on, McDougall got the Bobcat staff together to review progress; sometimes in his office, sometimes on board the private jet which was flying them to Valencia, Saarlouis, Bordeaux or Cologne, and sometimes at the test track at Lommel in Belgium.

McDougall let it be known that this weekly strategy meeting was to be an informal affair in shirt sleeves, but it was very serious all the same.

'What we must have on this programme is total discipline,' he told them right at the start. 'More discipline than you've ever known on any previous programme. We can't have any nonsense this time. It's a luxury we can't afford. In our normal programmes the cost of changes and putting things right after production has begun, can be as much as 18 per cent of the launch cost: redesigning components, sorting out the plant and

John McDougall, president and future chairman of Ford Europe, in conversation with the author.

tooling, small improvements to the product, changes in materials. This time we cannot allow more than 7 or 8 per cent. That means we've got to go all out to make sure that nothing goes wrong when we start to roll. I want everything to be perfect in all departments before production begins.'

The weekly conference over which McDougall presided was only one link in the chain of organisations which was set up to coordinate and control the programme. Some people had been in favour of handing control of the Bobcat project to special teams separate and distinct from the normal management structure. Bill Bourke wanted none of that.

'There would be too many problems integrating men and methods when the time came to start production. Everyone who has to design the car and make it must be involved in the whole programme right from the start. But clearly we should have some central body for control and coordination superimposed on the normal system.'

This was a chance for Erik Reickert to put into practice the latest theories he had brought over from his years at the Harvard Business School. He and his 'Incorruptibles', Bob Torkelson and Jim Capolongo, were to become the special controllers of the programme, the tireless commando which kept an eye on everything. Ford's system of financial control is reputed to be one of the best in the business. Reickert wanted to achieve the same degree of perfection in the operational control. New committees were formed of all those who had a direct responsibility for the programme and they met regularly, calling in any experts they needed. The Special Product Committee created in October 1973 and presided over once a month by Bill Bourke exercised overriding control and power of decision over all aspects of the programme.

Special launch committees met regularly, often on the sites of the new factories, to deal with engineering, fit and finish, plant and equipment, sales and marketing. Every two months the principal managers met for a general launch meeting with McDougall in the chair. The latest progress was checked against the fixed targets and working plans were drawn up for three to six months ahead in each area of activity.

Finally, the top management from Detroit, led by Henry Ford, joined the management of Ford-Europe every three months as an Executive Committee for a series of discussions and top level decisions covering strategy, finance, technical matters and government relations.

A strict and meticulous system of communication was set up which laid down the subject matter and frequency of the reports which were to be prepared in each area for the benefit of the central controlling body. Reickert himself composed a monthly action report for Detroit and every two months a status report gave a detailed account of progress.

In addition there were, of course, all the usual committees which meet at fixed intervals to decide the destinies of Ford-Europe with or without Bobcat: the Operating Policy Committee, which deals with a wide variety of different subjects; the Project Appropriation Committee which adjudicates on requests for new budgets; the Product Planning and Development Committee which is the ruling authority on the development of new vehicles; the Programme Timing Committee which makes sure that the timetables in operation correspond with the original plans; the Programmation Committee responsible for approving all the production programmes and the Sales Review Committee which reviews sales figures along with any other external or internal factor which may influence the company's commercial policy.

But even that is not all. There are also a Pricing Committee, a Product Reliability Committee, a Heavy Goods Vehicle Committee and others which need not concern us here. But from now on Reickert himself or one of his 'Incorruptibles' sat on every committee. Anywhere, at any time, some question involving Bobcat might crop up. They could not afford to miss a single one.

*

These then were the men, this was the organisation, this was the system. But the main thing was the foundation on which it was all erected. This is where the Bobcat project went further than any previous programme. Never before had the targets

156

been defined so precisely and in so much detail. In the beginning some of the 3,000 engineers at Dunton and Merkenich grumbled and snorted.

'These guys are real madmen! They are turning us into slaves!'

But they came to realise that the system had its good points. The basic rule was to take all possible precautions, including the investment of considerable amounts of money *before* the car was launched to reduce problems to a minimum afterwards, to avoid unpleasant surprises and increase financial returns to a maximum *after* the car is on the market.

On the technical and industrial side a Master Launch Plan was drawn up, distilled from all the experience acquired during previous new model launches. It defined all means and objectives. It provided engineers and analysts, controllers and managers with a permanent check list against which they could measure their progress and assess their own preformance.

Meanwhile the prototype itself was getting the treatment. The Red Book already established the financial and technical framework within which it was to evolve, but this was not regarded as sufficient. They decided to set up a continuous system of reports under 26 main headings; one person in each of these areas was made responsible for reporting regularly on what problems were arising and how the work was progressing. Among the subjects included in the list were a number of vital general questions: the timing of the programme (on the triple levels of product evolution, plant construction and supply of equipment), the state of negotiations with the various governments concerned, information on the projects and activities of competitors, forecasts of production volumes, financing and overall cost control.

However, the most important innovations concerned the car itself. Precise objectives were laid down, covering the car's running costs, performance, reliability, ease of maintenance, weight, finesse (including the level of equipment and the quality of the finish), complexity (which means essentially the number of parts in the car and the ease with which they can be put together), and warranty.

Further and from the start, they built bridges in the form of Feasibility Meetings to link the experimental engineers with the production engineers.

'It's not enough just to be ingenious, we must be practical,' said McDougall. 'When an engineer has devised a new component he must get in touch right away with the man who will have the job of making it. You can't be abstract. You must always find out on the spot whether the thing can be made, how it can be made and how much it will cost. If we check on this while the car is being developed we shall avoid lots of problems and needless expense when we start to put it into production.'

There remained the problem of organizing design and development within Ford-Europe, this two-headed giant. An assistant to Lou Veraldi, Dick Edwards, a former U.S. Marine, was the chief engineer of the programme. Under him were four men, each responsible for one 'system', that is a group of components: chassis and electrical equipment, engine, transmission, bodywork. The teams working on the first two systems were based at Dunton; those for the other two at Merkenich. And Ford-Germany had overall responsibility for the complete product, including crash and endurance testing which took Bobcat from the Lommel proving ground to the car-breaking tracks of Africa and the frozen roads of the Arctic.

'If there's the slightest carelessness on a programme as complicated as this, the whole thing can slip through your fingers,' said Bill Bourke 'But with the organisation we have set up now, at least we won't be walking the tight rope without a safety net.'

LIVING WITH LOGISTICS

'Oh, if only we could have that billboard,' said Abilio de Quiros, the P.R. man in Spain to his boss Carl Levy.

'Perhaps we could,' said Levy. 'Why not ask Coca-Cola?'

Opposite the exit from Valencia airport was a superb advertising billboard framed by cactus and palm trees, proclaiming the virtues of Coca-Cola. De Quiros, who went there regularly to welcome important visitors arriving on Ford's private jets would have been quite pleased to replace the famous bottle with the no less celebrated Ford oval, especially as Henry Ford himself was expected at Valencia in a few weeks for the laying of the foundation stone at the plant.

He got to work. Telephone calls, a word here and there, lunches, charm, chatting up, and a lot of persuasion.

'Of course, my dear chap, we'll install Coca-Cola slot machines everywhere in the plant! Coca-Cola in the canteen? Naturally there'll be Coca-Cola in the canteen! Besides, don't you remember the shape of the Taunus a few years ago and how people in Germany used to say it looked like a Coke bottle? Even our designers did you a good turn!'

When Henry Ford arrived at Valencia on 26 March 1974, accompanied by Caldwell and Bourke, the first thing to catch his eye, even before the government minister, the official escort and his Spanish management, was his own name, the name of his company, written in giant blue letters on a white background: 'Ford Valencia Welcomes Ford'.

This display board had a symbolic significance. From now on Ford was really becoming part of the Spanish scene. When Henry Ford ceremonially laid the foundation stone of the Almusafes plant, he was accompanied by the Minister for Industry, Alfredo Santos Blanco. The provincial governor had wished to keep the visit quiet but the news travelled fast.

Henry Ford at Almusafes: *'Moltes gracies!'*

When Henry Ford and his party arrived in the square in front of the Almusafes town hall, it was black with people, hundreds of them, who each wanted to shake Señor Ford by the hand.

'You must speak to them from the balcony,' said the mayor.

Henry Ford was enraptured.

'I must thank them,' he said.

'Don't just say *gracias*,' urged de Quiros, 'say *moltes gracies*; it's the local dialect.'

Henry Ford stepped forward and with a perfect accent he shouted: '*Moltes gracies!*'

There was a great outburst of applause. Several women crossed themselves:

'Did you hear? He speaks Valencian!'

Thanks to the mayor for all he had done for Ford. Bear-hugs, back-tapping.

'I would like to send you a personal present, Mr Mayor,' said Henry Ford. 'What would you like?'

'A photograph of the two of us, signed by yourself.'

The mayor was to get his photograph, of course, and hung it up at home.

'This is something that belongs to me, not to the town,' he said. 'It's something that I shall be able to keep when I am no longer the mayor.'

Soon aferwards another gift would arrive: a tie with the arms of Almusafes, which had been made specially in London's West End. From then on the mayor was to wear no other...

There was a full programme for the day. Inspection of the site, laying the foundation stone. Reception at the town hall in Valencia where the orchestra alternated 'Valencia! Valencia!' with the 'Stars and Stripes'. An official lunch followed given by the provincial governor in honour of Ford and the new steel foundry being built at Sagunto. There were speeches and press conferences.

Next day Henry Ford paid a brief courtesy visit to General Franco in Madrid. From Kosygin to General de Gaulle, from Kennedy to the Queen of England, there were few heads of state whom he had not met, long before his namesake in the White House began doing it on his own. In the Palace of La

162

Quinta he had a talk with Prince Juan Carlos whom he had already visited in his private residence of La Zarzuela. Juan Carlos, who speaks perfect English, was deeply interested in the motor industry in general, and in Ford's project in particular. He got on well with Carl Levy, president of Ford-Spain, both being members of the same yacht club. He turned out to be one of Ford's strongest supporters in Spain. Henry Ford then went to meet the head of the government, Carlos Arias Navarro. The same day, with the Minister of Labour, he publicly signed the agreement between the government and Ford for the technical training of the workers at Valencia.

In all, over 9,000 workers were to be employed at the Almusafes plant on engines, bodywork and final assembly, when production was running at full capacity. Four thousand of them were to be trained as skilled workers by the Spanish labour organization; the rest would be trained by Ford. The first courses, designed specially for maintenance personnel were to begin at Almusafes itself and in two neighbouring towns, Silla and Benifayo. The scheme was to be expanded later at various training schools in Valencia, Sollane and Quadasuar. Finally, some 80 Spanish specialists were to be flown to Cologne on a charter plane at the end of the year for a course of advanced technical training.

Even before they had taken any steps at all to recruit workers, Ford had received over ten thousand applications for jobs, and they kept coming in at the rate of 100 a day. Seven out of ten applicants lived within a six-mile radius of Almusafes but applications also came in from skilled workers born in Valencia who worked at SEAT in Barcelona, at Ford or Opel in Germany and Belgium, even at Volkswagen. There were 198 Spaniards employed at Ford's Belgian plant at Genk, 56 at Cologne, 8 at Saarlouis. Later on, some of these were to leave their foreign jobs and return home to become foremen at the Almusafes factory.

For the time being, however, the first priority was to recruit the inaugural team which would have to supervise construction and get the factories into action. The group was installed in temporary offices in the heart of Valencia until they could put a roof over their heads at Almusafes. It was a real United Nations. The chief construction engineer had been imported from Argentina. He had a perfect name to head a revolution, Horacio Liberatore, but he never destroyed anything. Quite on the contrary, he had to his credit the construction of several Ford factories in Latin America. He had another not unimportant asset: Spanish was naturally his mother tongue. The first personnel manager was a negro from Liberia. The president of Ford-Spain was an American transferred to Madrid after lengthy postings in Norway and France. As for the director of operations at Valencia, he was a 49-year-old German, Hanns Brand, a balding and rotund little man. His many problems would never blunt his sense of humour. He was one of Ford's top specialists in manufacturing and had successfully launched the Saarlouis plant four years previously. He was soon to beat some sort of air travelling record at Fords, with 120 flights in eighteen months between Cologne, Saarlouis, London, Bordeaux and Valencia.

They found him a perfectly well qualified secretary: she was Chilean, of German origin, and had received part of her education in the United States. Thoroughly trilingual, she admirably symbolised the Spanish project and made a valuable contribution to it.

There were other Germans in this original team, along with Americans, Britons, Argentines, Belgians, Dutch, Swiss and Portuguese, all of whom would eventually have to be assimilated into Spanish life and integrated into the Spanish organisations which were being built up in Madrid for administration and commercial affairs, and at Valencia for the industrial and technical matters. By the beginning of April 1974, Ford-Spain already had some sixty employees without counting the four buyers installed at Barcelona who were busy making the first contacts with future suppliers. All of them were studying Spanish on courses of at least 250 hours each, paid for by Ford. To weld all these individuals drawn from the most diverse backgrounds within the Ford group into a united and efficient team, they even called in a specialist Dutch institute which send sociologists down to organise seminars for the members of the staff. Among the subjects: 'How to behave towards the Spaniards.'

'They should also give the Spaniards a course on how to understand the Americans!' said Hanns Brand ironically.

The logistics officers got to work. There was the problem of housing the new arrivals, relieving them of all worries on this score and finding suitable schools for their children. This was no light task, since Ford-Spain would have 154 'imported' staff by 1976, and 65 of them would still be in Spain in 1979 on a permanent basis until enough qualified Spaniards could be found to take over their jobs.

Above: Hanns Brand, manager of the Almusafes factory: 120 trips in 18 months.

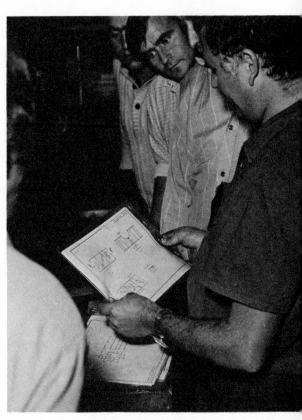

Right: Over two years before production, professional training sessions started at Almusafes.

The experts in Ford's central housing department embarked on a real estate market research programme worthy of a building contractor accustomed to operating on a world wide scale. They found for example that an appartment of 1,600 sq. ft. with three bedrooms cost 75,000 dollars in Germany, 48,000 in the United States, 37,000 in England and 51,000 at Valencia. With houses, the relationships were rather different. A six-roomed house of 2,700 sq. ft. would cost 200,000 dollars in Germany, 130,000 in England, 102,000 in Spain and only 90,000 dollars in the United States.

In the Valencia area there were some apartments for sale but few houses and still fewer to let. For the specialists who would be staying at Valencia for a relatively short time working on one of the various launch programmes (there would be 100 of them at most by 1976, and they were all due to leave by 1978) the problem was easily if not inexpensively solved. They would be put up in a new apartment block about nine miles from the plant, which rejoiced in the name of *Sol, Mar y Naranjas* (Sun, Sea and Oranges). Here they had to make do with a private beach, four swimming pools, several tennis courts, a restaurant, a self-service cafeteria, a laundry and a maintenance service. The annual rent for these apartments, forty of them, was between 1,700 dollars for a studio and 3,820 dollars for a four-bedroom apartment, all paid for by Ford.

On the other hand, to house the Foreign Service Employees from the International Division, some of whom would be staying for five years or more, a real programme of housing development was set in motion. A local developer was engaged to build sixty detached houses which could be sold outright to members of the Ford staff who wished to buy them, or leased from the developer by Ford who could then sublet them to Ford personnel at rentals which were fixed with an almost military regard for rank and seniority; houses worth 50,000 dollars for the humbler employees, rising to residences costing 98,000 for the top staff men. Financial assistance could be provided and certain expenses could be refunded over and above the cost of moving house. To avoid misunderstandings and subsequent arguments the terms were set out in great detail. The company would refund the cost of adjusting existing curtains, but new ones would not be reimbursed. Same for carpets. Certain essential items would be paid for, like waste paper baskets and electric plugs but no other domestic equipment. If necessary the purchase cost of a lawn mower might be refunded, but no other garden tools, swings or garden furniture! And it was to be understood that any such lawn mower remained the property of the company.

There's no limit to the situations you have to foresee in running a company which employs more than 450,000 people all over the world. You could easily find yourselves with enough mowers to take care of all the lawns in Central Park, the Bois de Boulogne and Hyde Park put together!

And then, the children. There is an anglo-american school at Valencia and Ford agreed to finance the construction of one additional classroom per annum for three years. The same was done for the German school at Valencia; ten children of Ford employees were to be enrolled there in 1974, sixty in 1975 and ninety in the peak year of 1976.

To provide the staff with cars for business use, some difficult negotiations took place with the Spanish customs authorities. Normally all imports of cars are forbidden except for a yearly quota of 250. It was only with great difficulty that Ford got permission to import 25 Taunus and Granada models for the Company's exclusive use, after paying a trifling customs duty of 126 per cent! They were followed by a further 150 on temporary importation. Customs duty on these was to be charged at the rate of 25 per cent per annum for four years, after which they would have to be re-exported. Meanwhile they must continue to carry German number plates.

'From 1977 on, everyone here will have to drive a Bobcat, including the president!' announced Carl Levy.

There was another problem: how to cope with the movement of personnel who had got caught up on the commuter roundabout, circulating between London, Cologne, or Saarlouis, Bordeaux or Madrid, Valencia or Belfast. There were those who had to attend the many meetings of the network of committees and working parties wherever they might be, and

167

they had to do so while losing as little time as possible. There were those who had not yet put down roots in Spain and who needed a chance to visit their wives and children from time to time. Not everyone has access to the executive jets, but Ford has a Travel and Reservations Office, which is both travel agency and airline.

Three Grumman Gulf-Stream 1 turbo jets are based on Stansted, the former Air Force base an hour's bus ride from the British Ford HQ at Warley and they run regular services. They fly five times a day out and back, between Stansted and Cologne, with up to 18 passengers. The journey time, door to door, from the Technical Centre at Dunton to the one at Merkenich is three and a half hours. There are four flights a week each way between Cologne and Bordeaux. Valencia-London runs every Tuesday with a return flight the following day.

But this was still not enough, so an 89-seater BAC 111 was added to the fleet. Before putting it into service, Ford had to change their own internal regulations. Up to then, not more than 18 company employees were allowed to travel in any one aeroplane, so as to eliminate the possibility of a major catastrophe if a plane crashed. From then on, the legal number was increased to forty: the BAC 111 was to fly every trip more than half empty.

As the number of travellers increased, so they needed more hotel rooms. By making block reservations, Ford were able to put their people into the best hotels in each city at very favourable rates. The rooms were reserved at the same time as the seats in the aircraft.

Put up in the best hotels, fetched and carried and sometimes fed too, helped in finding schools for their children, and houses to live in, what else was there for Ford's staff to do? The answer was, work! And in this area there was no one to relieve them of their duties and responsibilities.

*

Whatever else might be scarce in Spain, there was no shortage of problems, as the chorus of the concrete mixers began to accompany the waltz of the bulldozers on the 620 acres of Almusafes. There was for example the motorway by-passing Valencia, one branch of which was due to lead straight to the gates of the plant. Work on this *autopista* was moving very slowly. According to the official timetable it was not due for completion before the end of 1978. Repeated representations were made in vain in the hope of getting it finished during 1976, if not in 1975. It was going to be disastrous if the Almusafes area was to be torn apart by the construction of the motorway just as the plant was building up to full capacity.

And then there were all the problems of the infrastructure which had to be solved by Ford themselves, or in collaboration with the local authorities, before the plant could become operational; and they had to be solved today not *mañana*; 6 miles of roads and 7½ miles of railways to be laid inside the plant site and 27 acres of car and lorry parks. This involved moving 2.6 million cubic yards of earth, dynamiting 94,000 cubic yards of rock, pouring nearly 92,000 cubic yards of concrete and erecting 15,000 tons of steel beams and girders.

Some of the local environmentalists were afraid that the new plant would add to the pollution in the waters of the lagoon, so two experts were sent over from Detroit to investigate. They established that the waste water flowing out of the factory

A permanent aerial merry-go-round

169

would be purer than that which went in, purer in fact than the waters of the lagoon itself thanks to a purification plant which could treat 47,000 gallons of used water an hour.

The auxiliary installations were enormous. There were tanks to hold 1.1 million gallons of oil, several reservoirs for drinking

3.76 million sq. ft. of roofed space

water, industrial water and fire-fighting, compressors, an electric power station, 235 miles of cables, 135 telephone lines and 1,600 telephones. And of course the plant itself: an ultramodern factory with covered areas of 3.76 million sq. ft., 6.7 miles of overhead conveyors, 63 presses and, in the first

phase, 7,900 new jobs, all on a site which was still just a vast vegetable garden.

At Madrid, negotiations went on daily. Government officials worked with the utmost goodwill, but the Ford programme was so vast that even the best of the local experts got bogged down in their own regulations. Nothing could be imported free of customs duty except goods which could not be found in Spain, so they argued machine by machine, item by item, step by step. To get closer to the officials he had to deal with, Carl Levy set to work to learn Spanish, having already learned Norwegian and French in his two previous jobs. He did two hours in the morning, starting at 6.30 a.m., with a teacher who went to his home, and two hours after lunch, instead of a well deserved *siesta*.

Collaboration with the local authorities became more effective with every day that passed. A team from the postal administration, specially concerned with the problems of a high priority computer installation at Almusafes was flown to London and Warley to study Ford's requirements on the spot.

The port director of Valencia, from where the Bobcats would eventually be transported by sea to Italy and France went with Ford technicians to Antwerp to study how the Belgian port had solved similar problems.

Spanish customs officials toured the various European factories with Ford's own customs specialists. Their investigations led to a logical solution: the whole Almusafes plant was to become a closed customs area, with a customs office in the factory itself. This would make it easier for them to distinguish, car by car, what was on temporary importation, what was permanently imported, and what was destined for export.

*

However, the most delicate and most complex problem was that of the suppliers, and the formulation of a general policy on sources of supply. Bobcat was to be assembled in two factories, at Valencia and Saarlouis, and probably three after the addition of Dagenham to the list. For some of the vital components there was to be only a single source of supply, like Valencia for all the engines and Bordeaux for gearboxes and differentials. But could they rely on a single source for other items, the body pressings for example? And should they make sure of double sourcing for each of the components that were to be bought outside?

'In America,' said Iacocca, 'We do all the pressings in one plant, on one set of presses and we send the parts from there to the factories which assemble the cars.'

'Yes, but America isn't Europe,' replied McDougall.

About forty members of the Euro-American general staff were assembled in a large room at London's Grosvenor House Hotel. Ford's old London office in Regent Street had been sold and the builders had not yet finished converting the private hotel at 4 Grafton Street, former home of the first Baron of Brougham and Vaux, which was to replace it, so they were spending the day in a hotel reception room. Nine hours of tough, relentless debate. At one side of the room all the components of Bobcat had been laid out on trestles. Iacocca wanted to see everything, know everything and discuss everything. McDougall's team had gone even further for his benefit. They had built a miniature European goods train and put it alongside some American freight wagons built to the same scale.

'Why shouldn't we make all our pressings in Spain?' persisted Iacocca. 'It's cheaper to set up a single battery of presses in one spot and distribute the pressings by rail.'

'There are no tunnels in America, and there are few bridges. The bridges that do exist are very wide.' replied McDougall. 'Your wagons are enormous compared with those used in Europe. The useful load space on a European railway wagon is only 32 per cent of that on an American wagon. You can use enormous containers. Ours are minute by comparison.'

Iacocca and the team studied the models closely.

'And that's not all,' McDougall went on. 'Your trains are often three or four times as long as those in Europe. Transport costs are much higher over here. And besides, we have the problem of customs at the frontiers. And then there's the risk of unexpected hold-ups.'

So they looked into the figures, which had been prepared in great detail. It emerged that in some cases it could prove more economical in the long term to buy two sets of presses and press tools than to concentrate all the sheet metal work in one plant. The saving in transport costs would be greater than the outlay for the double investment, provided the same car was to remain in production for a minimum of ten years. This was the case with Bobcat.

On the basis of these calculations a compromise solution was finally adopted, 48 of the 99 Bobcat body pressings were to be double-sourced, at Valencia and Saarlouis. These were the biggest pressings, which posed the most difficult transport problems. The other 51 body pressings would come from a single source, Valencia.

And so the day went on with discussions and decisions, item by item. For example, sixteen components were to be produced 100 per cent in Great Britain. To protect production from hold-ups as far as possible, a stock of 40 days' supply was to be kept for each of these items, whereas the normal stock is 20 days' supply. Adding in the parts in transit at any one time, the total safety margin would be 55 days. But to achieve this they had to spend another 1.3 million dollars on extra storage space at Valencia while another 1.4 million of capital would be immobilised in the extra stocks lying idle.

The directors went on to settle a mass of details covering the whole range of bought-out supplies. Traditionally, Ford sticks to the principle of vertical integration laid down by Henry Ford I, who said:

'We should only buy from outside what we cannot make economically ourselves.'

This is why the founder of the dynasty had his own forests in north Michigan to supply the wood he needed, his own rubber plantations, his own foundries and his own glass works. Time has somewhat relaxed the rigidity of these principles and anyway, integration is much less developed in Europe. Therefore only 42.97 per cent of the total value of a Bobcat was to be produced by Ford. Of about 3,000 components in the car, 1,793 were to be bought from outside suppliers.

For this reason, Ford's arrival in Spain started a real gold rush among the component and equipment manufacturers. Besides creating more than 9,000 new jobs with Ford in Spain, the Bobcat project was destined to create another 10,000 in the accessory and component industry and a further 1,000 in the service industries. But things did not come along smoothly. Even though Spanish legislation had been amended, pressure from manufacturers already established in the country ensured that it remained unsympathetic to the setting up of new companies. Further the general economic recession was not exactly encouraging for new investments.

Finally, the draconian regime which Ford impose on their suppliers caused much grinding of teeth. Some of them, who had never previously worked with Ford, complained because the company would not grant them the long term contracts which they thought essential before expanding their factories.

'We keep faith with those who serve us well. Our past record proves it,' said Ford.

But there were many others who took fright at Ford's proposals on price and above all on quality. Ford were not content just to receive supplies, check the quality and send them back to the manufacturer if they were below standard. Their inspectors were to install themselves in the suppliers' own works and stop any defective supplies at source.

The Spanish association of equipment and accessory manufacturers raised the standard of revolt. Chuck Tennant, Ford's executive in charge of negotiations and contracts with outside suppliers had to get their representatives together for an animated working lunch and explain the reasons for Ford's strictness, before they accepted the rules, and then only reluctantly.

'Either our product will have the best possible quality, and your prosperity will grow along with ours, or we shall all sink together,' he told them.

Eventually they agreed. You don't refuse to take part in the production of 400,000 engines and 260,000 cars a year, even if it does involve some unaccustomed effort. Everyone realised that Ford's arrival was like manna from heaven. Already more than half of the money invested in the construc-

One week after Fiesta's production launch in Spain, King Juan Carlos and Henry Ford II officially dedicated the Almusafes plant, seen right ready for full scale production. The King was offered one of the first Fiestas assembled in Spain.

tion of the factories and their equipment was flowing into Spanish enterprises: 162 million dollars out of a total 338 million. Of the rest, 85 million dollars was going to German companies, 26 million to the French, 25 to the British and 24 to the Americans.

Spain had an even more important share in the supply of parts and accessories. One by one, the pieces of this gigantic industrial jigsaw puzzle were fitted into place. Some of the future suppliers were to be regular Ford suppliers who already had subsidiary companies in Spain which could be expanded as required; other suppliers were taking advantage of the Bobcat project to set up businesses in Spain and finally there were local companies which had never worked for Ford but were now ready to take the plunge.

In all there were 335 suppliers who were investing 300 million dollars, solely to meet Ford's immediate requirements. Ford's total purchases of parts and components during the early stages were estimated at 514 million dollars par annum, 52 per cent of which would go to Spanish companies.

Here too, multiple sourcing was decided upon in about 85 per cent of cases. It was too risky to depend on a single supplier, with the possibility of production being disrupted by his whims, poor quality in his supplies, or labour troubles in his factories. Because of this, the fall-out from the Bobcat would be felt right across the continent. Every year Germany was to provide supplies worth 160 million dollars, Great Britain 42 million, France 17 and Italy 4.

Then another precaution was taken which proved a windfall for the Spanish suppliers. To give them a chance to get their hands in, to gain experience and improve their quality, Ford didn't wait for the launch of Bobcat before placing the first orders. From 1974, some of them were asked to make parts for cars in the existing Ford range, which were sent from Spain to Germany, Belgium and England. These orders alone were worth 5 million dollars a year.

This was only a beginning. But some of those at the summit of the Ford hierarchy had begun to wonder whether it should not also be the end.

THE YEAR OF UNCERTAINTY

The quickest way from London to Detroit is the morning flight via Boston. Once again, Bill Bourke was on board, quietly installed in the hushed comfort of the first class section up front, well away from the hum of the jet engines. For him, as for all Ford's top executives, the aeroplane is a mobile office; a haven of peace, and the best possible place to study reports quietly, far away from the telephone, free from meetings, committees and conferences.

Bourke's thoughts strayed to his home on a faraway hillside in Australia. He went back there from time to time with his Australian wife, when they could manage to take a holiday. But during the summer of 1974, vacations were out of the question. The storms of recession had hit the motor industry, just as Bobcat, the baby lynx with the many parents, was coming to life.

A few days earlier, after a fresh look at all the factors in the programme, Bourke had decided to bring forward the start of Bobcat production at Saarlouis from 23 August, 1976 to 31 May. He felt that the rapid progress on the preparation of the plant justified the risk. The time available for preparatory work was thus reduced by three months in all sectors of the programme, but this acceleration would give the teams who had to move on from Saarlouis to Valencia an extra three months in which to prepare the Spanish launch with the benefit of all the experience they would have gained in Germany.

Above all it would allow the public announcement of Bobcat to be brought forward to 1 September, 1976. By then more than 26,000 of the new cars would have rolled off the assembly lines, enough stock to launch the car in Germany, France and Italy and to take advantage of the exposure which it would receive at the autumn motor shows in Europe.

Other markets would have to be supplied later, but these extra three months would be invaluable. Ford had already been waiting too long for their new small car, as the crisis was now demonstrating.

All this was going through Bourke's mind as he opened one of his folders. This was the case he was going to have to defend next day before Henry Ford and a worried Board. In Europe the Bobcat teams were working flat out, but in Detroit the mood had changed from reasoned enthusiasm to systematic doubt. The figures which Bourke was going to produce were not very encouraging. Fluctuating exchange rates, with the dollar plunging to its lowest level ever, had considerably reduced the possible profit ratio on the Eagle/Bobcat programmes. In March a conference on future production volumes had decided that as a result of the energy crisis less production capacity would be needed in the years to come. Even with Bobcat, Ford did not expect to make more than 1,425,000 new car sales in Europe in 1980 whereas before the crisis they had predicted 1,646,000 units. It began to look as if the new Valencia plant would not be able to operate at full capacity and this would further reduce the interest of the programme. In addition, the investments at Saarlouis were looking more expensive because of the unnaturally high value of the Deutschemark against the dollar.

'Is it still possible to stop the whole thing?' asked one of those present.

'You can always do it if you have to,' replied one of the finance men.

'Once the machine has started rolling you can't stop it,' said Henry Ford. 'The most you can do is to slow it down.'

The Board, as the general staff of the company, was worried about the recession in the car market, the finance men were concerned about rising interest rates and the general scarcity of money, and Henry Ford himself was beginning to doubt the prospects for Bobcat as a universal car. It looked as if it would be difficult to find the money to 'federalise' Bobcat and to build a South American Bobcat in Brazil as they had originally hoped. In this pessimistic atmosphere, Bourke fought tooth and nail to defend what had become his infant. He promised he would have studies done of possible modifications and perhaps curtailments of the programme and said he would try to make further economies in all areas.

'Unless we can get back to a reasonable return we must face up to the possibility of abandoning the whole Bobcat programme,' said the Board. 'This is no time for gambling.'

Bourke must come back with a better set of proposals.

'We shall expect you in October,' they told him. 'It'll be all or nothing.'

*

In London, Cologne and Valencia, imaginations and computers were put to work. Ford-Europe were quite determined that they were not going to be beaten by the recession and they had demonstrated their determination by reorganising the management of Ford at Cologne. In August 1974, Bob Lutz, 42, a former sales manager and director at Opel and then at BMW, became managing director of the German company. Born in Switzerland, Lutz was educated in the United States and served in the Marines as a jet pilot. With an excellent understanding of the German car buyer and a flair for dynamic and aggressive management, he quickly got his staff organised, enthused his dealers and caught the imagination of the public, to get Ford-Germany moving again. Better still, he took a profound personal interest in the products and exerted an invaluable influence on their development. A first class driver, he soon became Bobcat's most enthusiastic tester and critic.

He was one of those who were determined to save the little car at all costs and knew how to help. The report which Bill Bourke presented to the Board at the end of October proved decisive in this respect.

'You asked me to re-examine our programme from top to bottom. We've done it,' he said. 'We've succeeded in two ways; reducing the total cost of the investment, and at the same time increasing the return on the capital employed. As far as we could see in June, our return on capital was obviously inadequate. Our latest forecasts, I am happy to report, are in line with those you accepted when you approved the programme.'

The gentlemen on the Board sighed with relief. To present his case as clearly as possible, Bourke had arrived in Detroit with a box full of slides which he projected in the boardroon, with a running commentary.

As the foundation for his arguments, he analysed the evolution of the European car market. In 1973, before the energy crisis, A and B cars had taken 20.9 per cent of the whole European market and they were expected to reach 23 per cent by 1980. But from 1974 the share taken by these, the smallest cars, had risen to 26.1 per cent and only those manufacturers offering this type of car had been able to increase their market penetration; Fiat and Renault had each gained 1.4 points, while General Motors had lost 1.2 per cent, and Ford and Chrysler had each lost 0.8 per cent.

'We are convinced that this is a continuing trend so long as running costs keep rising as they are doing now. In 1975 it will cost a European motorist 40 per cent more to own and run a car than it did in 1973. This makes Bobcat indispensable for Ford in Europe. Without Bobcat, and without our Spanish plant, our share of the European market would be no more than 10 per cent by 1980. If we carry out the Bobcat and Eagle programmes, Ford's penetration will go up to 12.5 per cent, which means sales of 1,425,000 units, 365,000 of which will be Bobcats.'

Bourke went on to reveal the changes in the programme suggested by Ford-Europe, the savings they hoped to achieve, and the revised financial provisions dictated by the movements of the exchange rates and the economic recession.

The main proposals, based on the new forecasts of the overall production volume required, involved two measures; they would give up the idea of building the Taunus in Spain from 1978 onwards and they would abandon the proposed extensions of the Saarlouis plant. They would still have all the production capacity needed for Escort, Taunus, Cortina, Granada and Capri in the existing factories. The extra capacity freed at Valencia would be used to increase Bobcat output.

Purchase of a number of presses and some other low priority equipment was to be deferred. By confining Saarlouis Bobcat production to three-door models only, they could save three million. And renegotiation of the prices for the most important presses had produced further savings.

In all, the savings that were achieved amounted to almost 100 million dollars.

The overall profit forecasts for Ford-Europe were now less optimistic than they had been in 1973, but Bobcat offered a good hope of improving the situation. First of all, there were the latest forecasts showing that by 1980 Bobcat sales in Europe should be 25,000 units a year more than estimated.

Detailed analysis of the European national markets produced forecasts of 94,000 sales a year for Bobcat in the United Kingdom, 59,000 in Germany, 60,000 in Italy, 46,000 in Spain, 40,000 in France and 64,000 in the rest of Europe. Moreover, recent price increases made by Fiat, Renault and British Leyland in particular suggested that in future the prices of small cars would be rising faster than those of the larger vehicles. For a long time small cars had been sold in Europe at cost price, or even at a loss, and the manufacturers tried to make up for it on the medium and large cars. This tendency had now been reversed, partly because of the greater proportion of small cars in the total output, and also because the public were accepting new, more costly versions of popular small cars with more comfort, better equipment and higher performance. This evolution in public demand and the return to a more rational pricing policy was expected to improve the financial position of the Bobcat operation by a very substantial amount.

At the end of dozens of additions and substractions of this kind, Bourke presented the final bill:

'As you can see on these charts, we managed to sharply reduce our investment', he said, 'and our adjusted return on capital now goes back up to where it was at the beginning of our programme.'

Bourke also took the opportunity to report that the building operations at the Valencia and Bordeaux plants were on schedule and that some other clouds hanging over the programme had been dispersed, especially those concerning finance; the loans requested from various financial organisations in Europe were to be granted in the normal way.

Bourke had finished.

At the top of the table, Henry Ford spoke:

'I think we can be pleased with the work they have done in Europe. My view is quite clear. We are in Spain and we're going to stay there.'

The Board too were convinced.

'Go ahead!' they told Bourke, 'And let's hope you are lucky...'

*

While these anxious discussions were taking place, work on all aspects of the Eagle and Bobcat programmes had never been interrupted. Nevertheless that board meeting in October 1974 was for both projects a sort of re-birth. Had it been launched a little later, at the depth of the recession, Bobcat might never have seen the light of day. But as it was already a healthy infant by the time the recession began, it was able to weather the storm and emerge stronger than ever: Ford had never in their history needed a small car as badly as they needed one now. In the middle of the depression, the multi million Bobcat was perhaps a luxury and a gamble. But it was an essential luxury, an indispensable gamble.

Carl Levy, who had naturally maintained a low profile until then, invited Spanish journalists to a press conference on 28 October, his first in eight months. He reviewed the progress of the construction at the plant and he replied to criticisms regarding the use of Spanish capital to finance part of the programme. He reminded them that Ford would be exporting 170,000 cars from Spain every year, which would more than double the country's automobile exports. In addition, they would be sending abroad 180,000 engines a year. Ford's net contribution to Spain's balance of payments would be 21 billion pesetas a year from 1980 onwards, but it was already in credit even before production had begun.

184

'Our engine assembly line will start up on target on 26 April 1976,' he told them, 'and our first Spanish-made car will roll out on 15 November, 1976 at 8.30 a.m.!'

A few days later, a letter arrived on Levy's desk, accompanied by a cheque for 10,000 pesetas, drawn on the Banco Guipuzcoano de Bilbao. It was signed by one Rafael Matias.

'With the greatest respect it seems to me rather amusing that you should think you can fix the date and the time when your first car will be completed, 31 months ahead, however efficient your programming and your computers may be. I will take you at your word anyway. I enclose my cheque for 10,000 pesetas as a deposit on the purchase price of the first car to come off the assembly lines at Almusafes. I would like to be present to take delivery of the car as soon as it is completed and I should be grateful if you would let me know in due course the exact time when this will happen. Obviously I shall not hold it against you if you are a few days early or a few days late!'

Carl Levy replied immediately:

'We shall keep to our timetable and our first Spanish car will definitely be built on the morning of 15 November 1976. I have made a note of your order but I am returning your cheque. We shall arrange the transaction through your local dealer in due course.'

Then something happened which did not figure in any of the programmes or forecasts. On 9 November 1974, Ford-Spain's first football team, composed of employees from Valencia and Almusafes, played its first match and won.

'Now we really exist!' said Hanns Brand.

*

However, there is much more to selling cars than building a factory or showing the flag on the football field. You must be represented in every town and village and at every major crossroads to sell the cars and service them.

'You can set up a factory in two years, but it takes fifteen years to build a good dealership,' said Carl Levy.

As yet, Ford had practically no dealers in Spain, apart from the one who arranged temporary import sales to tourists and the four who distributed the meagre quota of 250 cars a year which Ford was authorised to import and sell in Spain.

By the end of 1974 another four dealers had signed exclusive contracts with Ford. Three of them had up to then sold Authis produced by the British Leyland subsidiary which had now ceased production and the fourth had previously handled nothing but used cars. Two years later, when the first Bobcats were to come off the production lines, Ford would need 70 dealers, rising to 110 by the end of 1977, 200 by the beginning of 1979 and 220 from 1980 onwards. Finding first class dealers was not easy, since Ford could offer them only one model while Spain remained outside the Common Market.

Even so, Carl Levy had already received 600 applications. He and his sales director, a transfer from Ford-Argentina, travelled up and down the country, meeting and sizing up the candidates. Some of them were excellent, like the Lincoln-Mercury dealer who had sold his business in California to retire to a less polluted atmosphere at Marbella and wanted to open a Ford dealership with Prince Alfonso de Hohenlohe. There were also Germans and Swedes who had retired to Palma de Majorca after a life time in the motor trade and were itching to go into battle again under the Ford banner.

There were others like the policeman in a village in the Asturias who had just retired and wrote:

'I haven't much money and I can't drive very well, but I know everyone in this part of the world. I have helped a lot of people in my lifetime and I am sure all my friends would buy cars from me. I would like to be your agent here. How should I go about it?'

A DIFFERENT CAR

On 6 November 1974, they were all there. Henry Ford, Iacocca, and a string of vice presidents had arrived from Detroit to join the European engineers in driving the first of the 'complete prototypes' of Bobcat. This one owed nothing at all to its competitors; it was a Ford down to the very last nut and bolt.

The Bobcat team had been given one year to get this prototype running and they had finished it in less than eleven months, by 28 October to be precise, so that the American general staff could drive it during their visit to Europe. To spare them the tedious journey to Dunton, Ford-Britain had looked into the idea of staging the tests on the greyhound racing track at London's White City Stadium but the track was not really suitable and it proved impossible to organise adequate security measures. The Bobcat secret had already leaked out; a participant at one of the market research clinics at Düsseldorf had managed to take some photographs and sell them to various magazines, *Autopista* in Spain, *Auto Journal* in France, *Auto Zeitung* in Germany. To avoid further leakages the tests of this prototype were therefore staged on the private and carefully guarded 1½-mile track at Dunton, close to Ford's technical centre.

Dick Edwards and Jim Donaldson had purposely had the prototype painted in a discreet pale blue so as not to influence the judgement of the testers. The object of the exercise was not to impress them with a strikingly finished car, but to get their opinions on the road holding, handling and comfort.

Henry Ford testing Bobcat: 'It's a great job!'

The first mechanical prototype; in ▷ fact, the first real Fiesta.

6 November 1974. The final prototype evaluated by Ford's top brass was 'Ford' to the last bolt.

Most of the competing cars were lined up alongside Bobcat: Fiat 127, Renault 5, and the Audi 50, the latest addition to the ranks. The testers moved from one car to another, comparing their good and bad points. Each of them was accompanied by one of the engineers engaged on the project who carefully noted down his every comment.

'Very good gearbox.' said Henry Ford after a few moments at the wheel.

G. Hartwig in the passenger's seat noted it down.

'Excellent driving position,' added the chairman. 'Pleasant steering wheel, well positioned.' Hartwig went on writing.

'There's still too much noise. You can hear the transmission. And there's a whistle outside at over 70 miles an hour.'

'This is only Proto Number 1, Mr Ford,' Hartwig replied 'We haven't really got down to the sound proofing. It'll be much better very soon.'

'No doubt. I'm very pleased with it. Even in its present form Bobcat compares very favourably with the Audi and you're better than Fiat or Renault.'

Lee Iacocca also considered that the Bobcat package was better than the Audi 50, but A. Guthrie sitting beside him took note of several criticisms from the president: excessive vibration of the steering column, gearshift stiffness between third and fourth, undistinguished appearance of the sun visors, and room for improvement in the instrument panel.

Phil Caldwell and Fred Secrest were also very favourably impressed, but they thought the rear seats were too hard and should have softer cushions, the wipers were too noisy and they were sure that the controls for the seat adjustment should be easier to reach.

Nevertheless, Caldwell was delighted as he got out of the car.

'It's the best number 1 prototype I've ever driven,' he said.

Iacocca added:

'Visibility is exceptionally good in every direction.'

And turning to Lou Veraldi, Ford said:

'You've got a technical concept there which is ahead of the Audi 50. It's a great job!'

190

The engineers at Merkenich and Dunton had really made some progress in eleven months. They had kept strictly to the basic concept handed over to them by Bobcat's first parents, but the prototype hardly resembled the concept car sent over from Detroit sixteen months earlier.

The changes which had then been brought to that pre-prototype would make a very long list. Right from the start at the end of 1973, radial ply tyres were adopted as standard equipment, a system of air extraction was added and seats with a more European character replaced those which had been moulded at Dearborn.

Then the Kent engine had been redesigned. Its overall length had been reduced by 1.2 inches, which produced a useful weight saving of nearly 15½ lb. while at the same time improving reliability and giving easier access to the clutch and gearbox. The bores of the Bobcat unit were 74 mm, against 81 on the standard Kent engine; strokes were 55.7 for the 957 c.c. unit and 65 mm. for the 1,117 c.c. Fuel economy had priority over performance, so the power outputs were restricted to 36 and 52 b.h.p.

Another fundamental change was made in March 1974 when disc front brakes replaced drums and the diameter of the wheels came down from 13 to 12 inches.

Lee Iacocca at the wheel: there was room for improvement.

Then in June came another important departure. It became clear that the revolutionary front suspension proposed in the original concept could not be achieved with the necessary guarantees of reliability. Hoesch, the soundest of the German suppliers, had studied the double torsion bars and their technicians reported:

'We cannot make it within the tolerances you propose. The system is ingenious and we shall be able to make it one day. But at present it involves an unacceptable risk.'

They therefore substituted a more conventional system using MacPherson struts. Unfortunately this took up more space, so spare wheel and toolkit, previously stowed in the engine compartment, had to be moved to the luggage boot at the rear.

In August an original and ingenious arrangement was adopted for the rear loading area. The fuel tank was mounted under the rear seat and two compartments were pressed into the floor of the boot. One contained the spare wheel and the other was provided with a lid and a lock which turned it into a miniature safe for the stowage of valuables. The feature of a fold-down rear seat backrest which gives a further increase in luggage space was henceforth adopted for all versions of the car with the object of simplifying the manufacturing programme and reducing the investment. The lift-up rear door was standardised for all markets except Spain and Italy.

This last decision was changed again a few months later when it was decided that all Bobcats would be built with three doors, while the original programme had provided for 60 per cent of sales to be two-door models.

Adding still further to the attraction of the car, it was decided to launch a Ghia version, more luxurious and refined than the standard model. A small car need not necessarily be crude and primitive. It must be practical, functional and economical but some buyers are willing to pay extra for more style, comfort and equipment. The Ghia version was designed for this market.

The general appearance of the car was now being finalised. The lines were refined and some dimensions slightly modified; overall length went up by half an inch and overall height was

BASE

While the technical development of the prototype went on, the design studios kept working on the interior architecture and decoration of the car's various versions, from the base model up to the Ghia luxury version. A small car need not necessarily be crude and primitive.

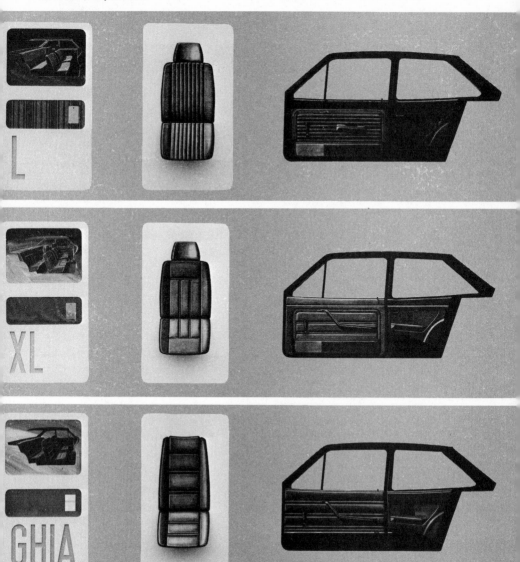

L

XL

GHIA

reduced by an inch although the height of the body had gone up by one fifth of an inch. A little extra space was gained inside the body; one fifth of an inch of shoulder width in front and two fifths of an inch at the rear. One fifth of an inch was added to front elbow room and rear headroom went up by the same amount.

'These are details, but on Bobcat, every little helps,' said Uwe Bahnsen, who was finalising all the aesthetic aspects of Bobcat at Merkenich.

'Cars are becoming smaller, but not the people who use them. Every fraction you can save is important.'

The designer's freedom of aesthetic expression is severely limited when he has to establish a shape for a car only 140 inches long—slightly longer than the Renault 5, or the Volkswagen Polo, but a fraction shorter than the Fiat 127 and the Peugeot 104.

'The problem is to give it an identity, a personality of its own,' Bahnsen added.

The design team succeeded. The glass areas on Bobcat were the largest on any car in its class; it was a real glass house. The general line was intentionally given a family resemblance to the new generation of European Fords which had started with the Capri II. The overall width, 61 inches at the centre door pillars, was greater than on any of its competitors, which could eventually make Bobcat a rival for some of the class C cars.

In general the lines were restrained and devoid of eccentricity, for they must not date quickly. And because these small cars, so similar in general layout, are mainly distinguished from one another by details, they had tried to find some new ideas; there was this miniature safe inside the luggage boot and they had also devised an easily removable sun roof for some versions.

A one-fifth scale model had already been tested in the wind tunnel at Aachen's Technical University but it was not until March 1975 after the real car had been tested in the full-scale Pininfarina tunnel at Turin that the decision was taken to modify the rear of the roof. The line was slightly straightened and rounded off at the end to form a tiny aerodynamic spoiler.

194

The Ford Model T and the Fiesta — years apart in design, but not in conception. Both cars were intended to bring motoring to as many people as possible. That the Model T did so is part of history. The Fiesta is the inheritor of that legendary past.

196

It was no more than one quarter of an inch high, but the sensitive balances of the wind tunnel showed that it was sufficient to improve the road holding and stability near the car's top speed, while at the same time achieving a slight reduction in fuel consumption.

And as proof that a prototype is a living thing, never frozen, but continuously evolving, another radical change was made in April 1975. Of all the parts of the original concept car, the only one remaining was the rear suspension. Bobcat still conformed to the basic concept and to the specifications on weight and cost laid down in the Red Book, but it now broke away from the original technical concept completely and became a 100-per-cent European car with a change in its rear suspension. The original suspension was soft, probably too much so, because there was a tendancy for the tail to drift sideways. It was now completely redesigned, with two longitidunal radius arms, a Panhard rod and a new rear axle.

Only thirteen months now remained before the first production car was to roll off the assembly lines and already the number 1 prototype had been written off in the first of the crash tests; a small matter of 330,000 dollars smeared over an unyielding concrete block. From now on only small detail improvements would be possible, but the battle went on to get the weight of the prototype down still further and to bring every aspect of the car up to the level of the best cars among its competitors.

For a long time the Fiat 127 had ceased to be the standard of comparison. Bobcat was now judged against the Audi 50 and VW Polo which had recently appeared on the market. The characteristics of each car were awarded marks from 0 to 10 and Bobcat had to be at least as good as the competition, preferably better, under every heading. Every step forward scored by the opposition led to an upward revision in the targets set for Bobcat. To equal the standard of the Audi 50 on noise and vibration, for example, would cost 8.50 dollars. The Red Book allowed only 3.50. Every time something like this cropped up, it was up to Ford-Europe's top management to arbitrate. The development of a new car is an infinite succes-

The cutaway drawing of the Fiesta shows how Ford designers have made the most of space. From the transverse engine to the petrol tank tucked away under the back seats, not a fraction of an inch is wasted.

sion of compromises, a process of evolving priorities. If they had to spend another five dollars here, could they save them somewhere else, or should they take a middle course? Because quality counts for so much, and because the competition is fierce, most of the compromises involved an increase in costs. In the end, it then seemed the production cost of Bobcat would work out at 43 dollars over the targets set out in the Red Book. But Bobcat would be something very different from a mini car, and they were not through improving it and increasing its production cost yet. . .

Fourteen complete prototypes were built for the exhaustive test programme and four others, with less complete equipment, were built for crash tests. They were all made by hand at a cost of between 90,000 and 100,000 dollars each. To keep the cost of the programme within bounds, there were some partial prototypes; the front half of a car for certain collision tests, for example. There were also 'mechanical prototypes'. These were bastard cars, consisting of a Bobcat platform, with all the correct mechanical parts, attached to a modified Fiat 127 body shell. They cost only about a quarter as much as a full proto-type and were perfectly adequate for testing the mechanical parts of the car. They had another valuable advantage; they could be tested on public roads and highways without being noticed by anyone! Sometimes complete cars of rival makes were used to test particular Bobcat components; the heating or the ventilation for example. In fact Ford-Europe became quite an important customer for their competitors. Before the full test programme had run its course, the Technical Centre at Merkenich had bought thirty-three Fiat 127, five Renault 5, four Volkswagen Golf, two Audi 50, two Volkswagen Polo, a Honda Civic and a Peugeot 104. More than half of them ended their careers in collision tests against a concrete block.

Veraldi kept tellings his engineers: 'We must find out where the competition have gone wrong so that we can do better. We shall be the last on the market, so we must be the best.'

Edwards for his part emphasised:

'There's only one way to make progress. You must contin-uously set up new challenges.'

Thousands of pictures were released throughout Europe to demonstrate how easy it is to operate the Fiesta's newly-designed sun-roof.

201

The versatility of the Fiesta's luggage capacity has also been emphasised. The boot has ample space for six pieces of baggage—but if you need to travel like a film star, just fold down the back seat, and pack away 15 cases!

Right: Keeping the Fiesta clean ▷
is child's play!

202

The roof car park of Rome's Hilton hotel was used to store away 100 new Fiestas to be driven by the Italian press on a long-term road test. Each car came with a bottle of Dom Perignon champagne.

Take weight, for example. The Red Book fixed a target of 1,580 lb. which was less than the weight of the Renault 5 and Peugeot 104, but slightly above the 1,547 lb. of the Fiat 127. In October 1973 the prototype weighed 1,579; by June 1974 they had got it down to 1,558.

'Weight is the enemy,' proclaimed Veraldi at the top of his voice and he should know, as he weighs about 220 pounds himself. 'Whether you're dealing with production cost, performance or saving energy, the first thing is to make the car as light as possible. My ideal would be to get it down to 1,499 lb. That sounds better than 1,500, doesn't it?'

They waged war on waste of every kind. Every possible ounce was hacked off relentlessly. Even sheet metal flanges which project after the spot welding had been done were systematically eliminated as never before.

Apart from weight there was a whole series of targets involving the appearance and the character of the car. In the beginning these had been fixed in relation to the Fiat 127 which was given 100 marks. On quality of paintwork for example, or the smoothness of the gearshift, Bobcat had to earn 105 marks. The arrival of the Volkswagen Golf had caused an upward revision in these targets, which became 109 for paintwork and 110 for the gearbox. The details of how all these targets evolved would fill several books; in fact the reports setting out how and why they were to be up-graded during the whole course of the programme filled more than 3,000 pages!

Everything was judged, weighed and measured minutely, not only against the competition, but against the other cars in the Ford range. Reliability was defined by the number of repairs per 100 cars needed over a period of twelve months or a utilisation of 12,000 miles per car. In 1973 they recorded 232 for the German Escort, and 291 for the American Pinto, figures which were appreciably below the motor industry average, but because they must and would do better, they fixed a target of 200 for Bobcat and then went further and reduced it to 180. Quality and reliability would be even more crucial since Bobcat was to be offered on many markets with an unlimited one year guarantee...

Above: The largest Ford produced in Europe—the Transcontinental with a 14-litre 6-cylinder turbo-charged engine developing 340 hp—was introduced to the smallest of them all, the 957 cc Fiesta developing 40 hp!

Right: Although small, the Fiesta is an ideal family car, and at holiday time it can tow a 400 lb caravan.

Promotion material included a 'do-it-yourself' cardboard model of the Fiesta, an 'encyclopaedia' on the car, a record, tons of description sheets.

The Fiesta is a truly European car, and whether it forms the subject of a British cartoon (above) or a German publicity picture (below), the emphasis is on the universal appeal.

Other proofs of the Europeanisation of the Fiesta: the publicity styles. Sensible in the Swiss manner (above) and sensual in the French (below)—national charac- teristics are diverted to make up the universal image.

Then there was the whole subject of running costs, including fuel, depreciation, insurance, hire purchase finance, taxes, service and repairs. For Bobcat they had to get down to 1,080 dollars per year in Great Britain (against 1,508 and 1,639 for its principal competitors). In Germany the figure was 1,525 against 2,174 and 2,313; in France, 1,571 against 2,154 and 2,169; in Italy 1,113 against 1,745 and 1,830 and in Spain, 931 against 1,446 and 1,458.

Could they really hit all these targets, meet all these challenges and achieve all these objectives? At least it would not be for want of trying, honestly, sincerely, enthusiastically, to achieve the best possible result, the best possible compromise between the demands of industry and the determination to give the buyers the best possible value for their money.

*

Ford-Europe had never let the depression blunt their enthusiasm, but their morale had received a tremendous boost from their triumphant launch of the new Escort at the beginning of 1975. It quickly established itself as a best seller. Would Bobcat be able to back it up with a similar success?

In the dog days of summer, 1975, two Bobcat prototypes went off to southern Morocco to run there in the blistering heat for three weeks. The following winter a similar expedition left for the Arctic Circle, braving the sub-zero temperatures in the northern parts of Sweden and Finland. Some circulated monotonously at the Ford proving ground at Lommel in Belgium, accumulating thousands of miles of endurance running. Others were twisted and shaken to destruction on the Merkenich test rigs, a battery of computer-controlled implements of torture. The engineers tested, checked, refined and improved everything which could still be modified.

Most of the presses and tooling had already been ordered and as fast as the helicopters put the roof trusses in place above the new workshops at Valencia, the machines moved into place. The first of them were installed in March 1975. Some 3000 construction workers were busy on the site and

Based on the Fiesta floor pan and using the running gear of the 1117 S version, the Corrida made its debut at the 1976 Turin show.

The Fiesta launch: thousands of press clippings for the automotive event of the year.

This 'four-in-one' concept car, the Prima, was developed by Ford Ghia operations in Turin, together with the Ford Design Center in Dearborn. It was based on the Fiesta and introduced at the 1976 Turin Show.

Fiesta production started at Dagenham in November 1976, and several thousand cars were exported to Continental Europe before sales in Great Britain began in February 1977.

already nearly 1000 people of 27 different nationalities had been taken onto the Ford-Spain payroll, ready to get production started.

Almusafes was becoming a new place for pilgrimage in Spain. Technicians came from the United States, Brazil and Australia to study what was being done there and to assess the possibility of making Bobcat in their own countries.

The whole Board arrived there in June, after stopping off at Madrid, to take a look at 'the biggest building site in the world' and then went on to Lommel to drive 'the smallest car ever built by Ford'.

From being an agricultural village of some 4,000 inhabitants, Almusafes was rapidly growing into a town. New businesses sprang up, and several banks had opened new branches. By the nineteen eighties, the town was expected to have 25,000 inhabitants. To record this evolution and dissect it, a professor of sociology from Stanford University had already moved in from California and started to collect data. Almusafes would soon be providing the material for a thesis and then another book.

When at last he was able to take possession of 'his' plant, Hanns Brand had two relics mounted on a plinth at the entrance, symbolising the past of Almusafes for those who must build its future. One was an old plough which had been found abandoned on the land where the factory was built; the other was an orange tree which had been torn up as the site was cleared. It had been chromium plated to eternally preserve it for posterity.

RETURN TO AMERICA

'We still have two weeks to change the car, haven't we, Bill?' Bourke turned to Bill Hayden. Tall and lean, with his hair falling over his forehead and spectacles perched on the end of his nose, Hayden looked rather like a clergyman.

'Two weeks?' he bounced back. 'Your two weeks were up a month ago!'

He was in charge of manufacturing. Valencia and Saarlouis were his, with the responsibility of installing the machines and conveyors, and launching the production of thousands of separate parts according to a strict and complicated timetable. At 46, he was the first British vice-president of Ford-Europe. He had gained his reputation for drive and organising ability in commissioning the automatic transmission plant at Bordeaux, the most successful plant build-up in Ford's history. He was the one who had persuaded the management that they should not join up with Fiat to produce the Bobcat transmissions in Spain, but should make them at Bordeaux.

'If you go on changing everything, I shan't get Bobcat out before the year 2000,' he said.

Hayden and Bourke were sitting side by side in the Ford jet which was taking them to the proving ground at Lommel. It was Tuesday, 9 September 1975 and they had left Stansted at dawn to meet the whole Product Committee assembled in Belgium. They were to spend that night in Frankfurt, where the Motor Show opened next day.

'Bill, I promise you there won't be any more changes after those we are going to make today.' said Bourke. 'But we must give the proto a last going over with a fine-toothed comb and add a few finishing touches.'

'Yes, I know,' said Hayden. 'But don't make it too hard. Most of the tooling has been ordered and I should be starting up the first production operations next week. If you change everything, the suppliers are going to curse you and my chaps at Saarlouis, Bordeaux and Valencia will want to cut my throat.'

'We shan't change everything,' he was assured. 'But we'll have to take another look at a number of things.'

In his briefcase, Bourke carried the latest reports of the specialists who had checked out Bobcat against the latest version of the Volkswagen Polo in three successive clinics. Looking at the two cars side by side in Germany, different groups of potential buyers had given favourable verdicts on Bobcat, but Volkswagen's latest model had come out best in a number of details. The task was now to up-grade Bobcat as necessary to put it ahead of its latest rival.

'The public already prefers Bobcat to the Fiat 127 and the Renault 5', declared Bourke as he opened the Product Committee meeting, 'but with the arrival of the Polo we are involved in an entirely new contest. We now have a first class reputation in Germany and we must protect it. We mustn't give anyone the slightest cause for criticism when we launch our new car. This meeting is vital. Today, we can still modify the car. Afterwards it will be too late.'

The technical tests which they had carried out on the proving ground that morning had been entirely satisfactory, except for a small amount of roll which had not been completely eliminated by the new rear suspension. Veraldi therefore proposed the adoption of stiffer rear springs, to be backed by an anti-roll bar on the sporting versions of the car. Agreed.

'We must do more,' said Bourke. 'We are also going to fit the most expensive rear seats on all models. We must have something more comfortable, with more padding. In front, the seats we planned for the middle range models must also go on the cheapest versions. And the front passenger's seat is to be given a sliding adjustment on all models. Everything must be right, even on the basic version.'

The others sitting round the table made notes. One engineer muttered to his neighbour:

'The bastard! For two years he's been driving us to save

ha'pennies here, there and everywhere. Now he's going to empty the whole cash box.'

Bourke sensed the meaning rather than heard it, and he smiled.

'It's because you've worked so well up to now that we can take these decisions today. The first thing we had to do was to make a car which would be impeccable technically and a reasonable financial proposition. Now we can add the finishing touches, the extra quality and style which will make it the most attractive thing on the market. Public taste is changing; tomorrow's small cars will be more comfortable, better equipped, and more expensive. We have to go along with it. The time has come to spend the money which you've been saving up to now.'

Several coachwork and interior prototypes had been brought from Cologne to Lommel in a covered truck to help the committee to crystalise their ideas and make their decisions. Among the modifications suggested by the Car Product Planning Office after comparing Bobcat with competing cars, was one to the lift-up rear door. From the start, this had been mounted on visible external hinges like the one on the Fiat 127. On the other hand, the Renault 5 and the Volkswagen Polo had concealed hinges. Like everything else, this problem had been analysed in a detailed report. External hinges, besides looking rather unattractive, can cause deterioration of the bodywork. The technicians explained that if the hinge attachments are done up too tightly they can cause ripples in the roof panel. There is also a risk of cracking the paint round the hinges when the tailgate is adjusted during final assembly, after the body has been painted. Moreover the fitting of a vinyl top on models where this applies is complicated by the cutaways round the hinges.

Concern for quality, ease of manufacture and aesthetic considerations all argued in favour of concealed hinges. However, this made it necessary to fit a second gas strut to eliminate the risk of twisting the tailgate as it was closed, which could later cause leaks round the edges. The point where the shoe pinched was that this extra gas strut put up production cost by 2.64 dollars a car, and added 512,000 dollars to the investment.

Endurance testing was carried out in secret on the private testing ground at Lommel, Belgium, but also on Scandinavia's icy roads and on dust tracks in Africa.

'Let's take the plunge!' said Bourke 'Whatever it costs, we can't afford to take risks at this stage.'

Another important decision involved the external appearance of the car. The original radiator grille was a sort of rectangular box with a chromium frame set in between the headlamps. It tended to make the car look narrow at the front and at various clinics the public had shown that they were conscious of it. The new front, produced by designers under Jack Telnack and Uwe Bahnsen, comprised a grille with clean-cut lines like a venetian blind, extending across the full width of the nose, giving it a much bolder appearance, more powerful and more modern. The slats were shaped like aerofoils, giving another advantage: the air was guided to the radiator more efficiently and the cooling was improved.

Modifications were authorised to raise the power output of the basic engine from 36 to 40 b.h.p. to give the cheapest Bobcat a more competitive performance. They also decided to be more generous with the tyres, fitting radial ply 145 SR instead of the 135 SR originally specified. For good measure, Bourke decided to standardise laminated safety glass, a heated rear window, inertia reel safety harness and a hazard warning flasher on all models.

The instrument panel, which was considered inferior to that of the Polo was replaced by another which had a matt silver insert round the dials to give it a richer appearance. Even more important, the principal hand controls were removed from the instrument panel and mounted directly on the steering column in the manner made popular by Mercedes-Benz.

'We don't often spend that much money in one day!' said Hayden, laughing.

'Right. Around 60 dollars a car in direct production cost. That means about 30 million dollars a year, but it'll be worth it. We now have nobody to fear for quite a while.'

The buyers would give the final verdict, but one more clinic held at Hamburg three days later supported Bourke's optimism. Some 180 potential B-car buyers were invited to assess Bobcat in its final form against the Polo. The two cars which they were shown were both painted red and both carried the same Volkswagen badge so that no marque image should influence their judgment between one and the other. The Bobcat prototype had already been given all the improvements decided upon by the Product Committee at Lommel and they hit the bulls eye first time. A few weeks earlier, in a clinic held at Frankfurt, the previous Bobcat prototype had been judged equal to the Polo in external appearance, but inferior in its interior arrangements. This time Bobcat won on both counts. It was only beaten on a few details: the shape of the bonnet (which Ford decided not to change because it reduced the wind resistance), the appearance of the rear lamps and the steering wheel, and the comfort of the rear seats which could not be improved to any extent because of the fuel tank underneath.

Apart from these points, the verdict of the clinic could not have been more encouraging. Bobcat was voted more original, more elegant, more modern, safer, more sporting and more economical, by a very large margin. Asked what they thought would be the difference in price between the two cars, those present estimated on average that Bobcat should cost 151 dollars more than Polo, which obviously delighted the Ford executives. They were further enchanted to learn that 72 per cent of those who filled in the questionnaires would prefer a Bobcat if the two cars were on offer at the same price.

Even if some of those taking part in the clinic might have changed their minds after a proper test run, which obviously none of the technicians was prepared to believe, Bobcat was now ready to take the great plunge.

*

Very soon it must also be ready to take a great jump across the Atlantic. Only four days after the Lommel meeting which finalised the last details of the European Bobcat, Henry Ford II let it be known during a press conference that the new baby car, conceived originally in Europe, then developed in the United States and ultimately matured back in Europe might cross the Atlantic once again to appear on the American market in a 'federalised' version. The news caused quite a stir in the United States. The press commented at length on Henry Ford's frank admission that his company might have been wrong about the impact that mini cars would make in America and that Ford had been slow to appreciate the chances of small European cars on the American market. But Ford, as the near future was going to show, had not been quite as wrong as some thought. Small cars were not yet in the U.S. to stay...

General Motors had stolen a march on Ford by deciding to build the Chevette in the United States, a conventional front-engine rear-drive car created by Opel and Vauxhall from existing components. The economic recession and high fuel prices were temporarily helping the importers. One in five of all cars sold in the United States was of foreign origin. The Japanese were wreaking havoc on the American market, especially in California, where foreign cars had become almost as popular as those from Detroit. The Volkswagen Golf, sold as a 'Rabbit' in the U.S., had taken over from the Beetle. Beside their American Chevette, G.M. were planning to import the Gemini built by their Japanese associates, and Chrysler were selling Mitsubishi Colts while preparing to launch an American-built small car based on the Simca 1307/1308.

However, Ford was not as far behind as it appeared. Right from the start, Bobcat had been planned as a possible 'universal car' and during the development of the prototypes everything had been done to make it easy to 'federalise'; that is, to adapt it easily to American standards on safety and pollution.

Everything had been foreseen and worked out down to the last details, at least in theory: the technical modifications required, the interior changes needed to give the car a more American character, the optional equipment, the selling price and the annual running costs, including depreciation, insurance, financing, taxes, service and fuel. Costing studies showed that if Bobcat was sold in the United States in 1977, the basic federalised model could well compete with the Volkswagen Golf-Rabbit

224

A 'federal' version of Bobcat, equiped with bumpers and lateral protections con-
forming to American regulations, was developed in parallel with the European version. Bobcat would soon be ready to cross the Atlantic.

and the Pinto, smallest of the American Fords. The running costs of the three cars were roughly the same. Production planners had worked out that the car would be assembled from 444 components for 49 American states but would need 456 in California because of that State's stricter pollution limits.

A plan for development and manufacture was ready, providing for the first American model to come off the line at Saarlouis on 31 January 1977, followed by an official launch in the United States that spring or summer.

Not a word or a figure was missing from the dossiers on the plan; it only remained for someone to give the engineers the go-ahead. If this decision was delayed, it was because Henry Ford still mistrusted the capricious and volatile American market. Bobcat had a lot in its favour. More compact than the Rabbit, it nevertheless had comparable internal dimensions and it was functionally superior to G.M.'s Chevette. But could anyone be sure that the American public would remain faithful to cars as small as Bobcat for a long time? Baby cars had been taken up enthusiastically in 1975, but would they still be making the running two years later?

On 11 September, two days after the Product Committee put the finishing touches to Bobcat at Lommel, the Board met at Dearborn.

Everyone was worried about the arrival of the Chevette on the American market, but Henry Ford remained calm.

'All the work that General Motors is putting into launching a small car on the American market must be good for us,' he said. 'When Bobcat arrives, the right climate will already have been created. People will then realise that our car, less conventional than theirs, is a better package.'

But was this a good enough reason to justify assembling Bobcat in the United States or perhaps manufacturing it there completely as General Motors had done with the Chevette?

'Don't let's rush it,' said Henry Ford. 'If you agree, we'll start with cars imported from Saarlouis. Europe can let us have them, starting in 1977, and we'll be able to see how the American market reacts.'

'That sounds very reasonable,' said a voice.

'What we propose in effect,' continued Henry Ford, 'is a holding operation which will give us time to study the market and think about it. Now that the dollar is getting stronger we can afford to import the car. Later on we'll be able to see more clearly whether it would be worth the risk to also make it over here.'

The Board unanimously accepted this plan. Once again this passed the buck back to Europe where it meant that the whole project, so recently curtailed, must be expanded once more with intensified urgency. The planned 400,000 units a year must suddenly be pushed up to 500,000. On engines, there was no problem. The American version of Bobcat could not use either of the engines produced at Valencia. It would have to be fitted with the normal 1.6-litre Kent engine made at Dagenham, where all the required capacity was available. Engineers at Dearborn were immediately given the job of adapting this engine to the onerous American emission standards.

With the gearboxes and front axles the problem was more difficult. Capacity of the Bordeaux plant had to be increased by 100,000 units a year immediately. Bordeaux II had to be enlarged even before it was finished. Counting in the normal automatic transmissions, the Bordeaux plant now had a capacity of nearly a million transmissions a year, which makes it one of the biggest specialist production units in the world.

Saarlouis and Valencia together can produce close to 400,000 Bobcats a year; Dagenham was to make the rest. On 17 September, Ford of Britain announced that it would be taking on an extra 1,000 workers in 1976 to begin producing a new front-wheel drive small car by the end of that year. The initial production was to be 300 a day building up to 100,000 a year. One side effect was that British production of Granadas, which was no more than 50 a day, was terminated and production concentrated entirely in Germany to free the space needed to build Bobcat.

'With good news so hard to find in the motor industry at the moment it is heartening to be talking about new models and new jobs', said Terry Beckett, the chairman of Ford of Britain.

The possibility that Bobcat might one day be built in Britain had been kept in mind right from the start. The decision to import the car into the United States merely speeded up the project. However, Dagenham was to be working for America only indirectly. Engines made in Britain would be sent to Saarlouis to be fitted into cars built there for the American market. Dagenham's main Bobcat output was to be right-hand drive models for the British and Irish markets.

Once again the engineers went flying round Europe moving the pieces on their giant board. Spanish engine production was provisionally cut by 50,000 units a year, but output of all other parts which Spain was contributing to the three European assembly plants was increased by 20 per cent. Bordeaux now had to plan the production of two different front axles: the European one and an American version reinforced to withstand the greater torque of the 1.6-litre engine. Thanks to sound planning the two versions had been developed side by side right from the beginning. In the same way, the Bobcat body had been designed so that the lateral reinforcements required by American legislation and the bulky federal bumpers could easily be fitted.

The Ford-Europe executives were rubbing their hands. The decision to import Bobcat into the United States made it very much easier for them to plan future developments of the European range. There was little need to spend time developing sportier versions of the European engine; the Kent 1.6-litre engine and transmission would do instead. And as Bobcat sales expand in the United States, Ford-Europe would most probably one day inherit an automatic transmission developed for the American version. Ford's market for such a transmission in Europe had been estimated at 20,000 units a year, which was far too small to cover the cost of development and production. Eighteen months earlier, Ford tried to get Fiat to collaborate in developing a joint automatic transmission which could have been made for them in England by Automotive Products, but Fiat was not interested and the idea was dropped.

Even before the first Fiesta rolled off the line, futuristic versions of the car were developed by Ford's design studios. Most of them will never see the light of day.

The federalized version of the Ford Fiesta, at first to be imported from Europe, has some 500 different parts to comply with American market conditions.

So even before the first Bobcat was born, a whole string of offspring was being planned, still more powerful, more elaborate and more attractive, and a great travel programme was being prepared for them. After the United States, perhaps Brazil, South Africa, Australia and New Zealand.

*

Exactly as foreseen in the programme two years earlier, the first preproduction engine came off the assembly line at Valencia on the appointed day, 22 September 1975, six months before the start of full production. It already incorporated 85 per cent of regular production parts, which was an advance on the original timetable. McDougall, Hayden and their staffs went to Valencia specially for the event and gaily greeted the firstborn at the end of the assembly line. At Bordeaux, the same day, the first front axle emerged from the new plant, also on schedule. A few weeks later, on 17 November, Veraldi's engineering department gave the green light for the acquisition of the final tooling and for the issue of firm orders for all the bought-out components. A month later, on 15 December 1975, Bobcat was transferred from development to production.

Bobcat was now frozen. No further change of any importance could be made before 'Job 1', that is before the first car came off the assembly line, except perhaps last-minute adjustements shown to be necessary by the endurance tests which were still going on, or some possible urgent modification which would have to be the subject of a dramatic document, a 'pink sheet', in the event of a major casualty. Only the top management can authorise this, postponing the start of production if it proves to be necessary.

But for the time being the tendency, quite on the contrary, was to speed up the start of production. Manufacturing reported to the chairman:

'We now have sufficient confidence in the car and in the progress of our work on the infrastructure to suggest that the start of production at Saarlouis be brought forward three weeks to 10 May 1976.'

Production would begin on a pilot basis, with a running-in period to train the workers on their new jobs. On 1 March 1976 the first series production engine came off the line at Valencia and the first regular production front axle was built at Bordeaux. The first complete car was to be assembled at Saarlouis in May and Almusafes would celebrate the birth of its first Bobcat not on 15 November as planned, but on 18 October—also one month ahead of schedule.

Any detail modifications found necessary would be held back until 90 days after 'Job 1', so as not to interrupt the running-in of the assembly operations. After that they were to be introduced progressively.

'Normally, you must reckon on about a thousand changes of one kind or another during the first year of production,' said Bill Hayden.

A car is not an inanimate object; it is a living thing in a state of perpetual evolution.

CALL IT FIESTA!

And now, what name were they to give the new baby?

The prototypes were running and the factories were getting ready to start the assembly lines rolling, but the car still had nothing but a code name, which it had been given long ago in the autumn of 1972, three and a half years before it went into production. Three and a half years that seemed like a century.

The people who originally worked on the concept car now barely remembered it. They had designed many others since and they were now developing prototypes for the nineteen-eighties. Those who lived with Bobcat had got so accustomed to the temporary name that they were in no hurry to find another permanent one. Some of them would have been happy to retain the original name tag. Bobcat sounds right, even if the word means very little to people in most parts of the world, but meanwhile Mercury had launched their own Bobcat on the market, and this had nothing in common with the little European car, so another name had to be found anyway.

In the Spring of 1974, Ford's marketing staff mobilised executives throughout Europe to compile lists of suggested names. What was needed was a short word, easy to pronounce, preferably with a continental flavour, easy to combine with the Ford name, and understood everywhere. It must have the same meaning in all languages, it must be original and pleasant, and for good measure it must be simple, credible and apt, suggesting the image of a small and economical, but also lively and sound car. And finally it must be a name that was not owned by anyone else!

Searching for such a name is like looking for a needle in a haystack. Nevertheless, a pile of suggestions arrived and a team of experts reduced them to fifty, then to thirteen. The choice was thus narrowed down to Amigo, Bambi, Bebe, Bolero, Bravo, Cherie, Tempo, Chico, Fiesta, Forito, Metro, Pony and Sierra.

An inquiry was launched to find out just what impression these names made on people. It was not conclusive. Ten per cent of those consulted confused Sierra with Siesta. Amigo, Fiesta and Sierra seemed too closely associated with Spain to fit a car which was to be produced all over Europe and perhaps all over the world. People on the continent thought Pony sounded very British, but the British didn't like it. Bambi, one of the most truly international names, left the Germans cold.

This investigation reduced the choice to five names: Fiesta, Amigo, Bambi, Pony and Sierra, but no one at Ford was enthusiastic about any of them.

'Apart from Escort, all our vehicles are named after a town or a region', said Bill Bourke. 'Taunus, Cortina, Granada, Capri. What we need is a nice name of a town. What would you say to Nice?'

'In German, it's Nizza' he was told.

'Well, couldn't we find a good German name? Like a glamorous winter sports resort, for example?'

'Something like Garmisch-Partenkirchen?' asked Bob Lutz, with a very straight face.

It was decided that the name finally chosen must be approved by the high command on 18 November 1974. Of all the countless important dates laid down in the programme, this was the only one which would not be adhered to!

Choosing a name for a new car is no simple matter. It is not just a question of digging out a word which makes the right impression on people in all the countries where the car is to be sold. Some names have had to be changed in certain markets because they had unfortunate vulgar meanings in the local language, which had escaped the notice of manufacturers who were not sufficiently good linguists. But the worst shocks can come from commercial interests. The town council of Cortina gave a banquet for Ford directors when the name of their resort was chosen for a new Ford model and the local council at Granada sent a gift to Henry Ford to commemorate the launching of the Ford Granada, but there were also some awkward customers who made life difficult.

When the Granada was launched in Britain, Lord Bernstein, chairman of Granada Television, wanted to sue Ford for using the name without his permission. Nobody at Ford had given a thought to his television sets when the car was christened.

The Mustang is known as such everywhere, except in Germany, where the name had already been registered by a company unconnected with the motor industry. The German owners of the name proved so uncooperative that the Ford Mustang is there known simply as the Ford P5, or Ford P7 for the latest model. Presumably P6 was omitted because P76 was the name of a British Leyland disaster in Australia.

In 1975, when Ford wanted to emphasise the economy of the models at the lower end of their American range by using the initials M.P.G., Henry Ford personally had to get permission from the Maine Potato Growers!

In fact choosing a name, making sure that it does not belong to anyone else and protecting it for the future, is really a job for lawyers. And Ford's lawyers were nervously marking time, waiting to hear the name which they would have to confirm and protect; the publicity men who were to launch the new car were becoming impatient and the marketing men who had to test public reaction to the new name could not wait to get started. But Bobcat was simply refusing to be pushed aside or lie down and die.

'Let's just call it the Model B,' suggested Walter Hayes, but he got no support at all.

Then one day, while they were sipping an *orange pressée* waiting for the Valencia-Madrid aeroplane to leave, two of Ford's public relations experts, Bob Sicot and Abilio de Quiros went over the list again with several of their colleagues. Immediately one name struck a chord with everyone: Bravo. It begins with a 'B', like Bobcat, it's short, direct, international. It is commonly used in the aeronautical alphabet. In Spain, Bravo is the name of a very courageous kind of bull, and everywhere the name suggests applause and enthusiasm. Bravo Ford! Ford Bravo!

'You can do anything with Bravo in any language in the world' said Sicot.

So Bravo came back into favour. Via de Quiros and then Levy, Spain whispered 'Bravo!' to Bourke. Via Sicot and then Hayes, the continent too said 'Bravo'! It began to look like a popular vote and Bourke became accustomed to it as a possible name for the new infant. He put the lawyers to work on a revised list of five names: Bravo, Fiesta, Amigo, Strada and Pony, in that order. They had to find out who, if anyone, had registered these five names and whether it was possible to obtain the exclusive use of any of them for the new car. The answer was not long in coming.

'There are only minor problems with Bravo,' reported the researchers. 'The name belongs to an Italian spaghetti manufacturer, but he has no objection to our using it. We hear that Lamborghini is thinking of using it on a new car, but that should not raise any problems for us. Fiesta is a different matter. This is a name which was once used by Oldsmobile and we would need to get permission from General Motors. Amigo and Strada raise no great problems. As for Pony, this is a name we registered some time ago. A South Korean manufacturer is using it at present but the car will only be sold in the Far East.'

Market research gave equal marks to Bravo and Fiesta. After consulting Bourke, Caldwell sent a note to Henry Ford. He explained that the people in Europe preferred Bravo, but made it clear that Bravo, Fiesta or Amigo would be equally acceptable to the management of Ford-Europe.

'We await your decision during October at the latest,' said Caldwell. 'We have to design the badges, prepare the tooling and launch the publicity campaigns. We are running out of time.'

Henry Ford sent a telephone message in reply.

'I'll give you my answer before then. But don't send me any more suggestions.'

Ford's European competitors tend to give their cars numbers based either on engine capacity or on design project code numbers, whenever this number is not selected more or less at random. Ford however have always tried to give their cars a personality by using a name rather than a number. Usually name picking has been Henry Ford's personal business. In an interview to the *Detroit Free Press* the Chairman made the position clear.

'We haven't formed any committee to christen the new model. I shall choose the name myself. There are always arguments about names for cars. Everyone has his own idea and wants to force it on everyone else. Last time I let them convince me, and we chose a bad name. This time I'll decide myself.'

Henry Ford shut himself in his office on the twelfth floor and started pacing up and down, reciting the suggested names aloud.

'Bravo... Bravo... That's no name for a car. Maybe it's all right when you say it in Spanish or Italian, but it doesn't mean a thing in English.'

Then he tried Fiesta. He liked the alliteration. Ford and Fiesta go well together. It's gay colourful, dynamic. He called Caldwell.

'Bobcat will be called Fiesta,' he said. 'You can tell Bourke.'

'But we must get permission from General Motors.'

'I'll ask them myself if necessary,' said Henry Ford.

He did. He called Tom Murphy, G.M.'s chairman.

'You want Fiesta?' Murphy said. 'You can have it. It's yours!'

And so the smallest Ford of modern times was called Fiesta. Caldwell told Bourke on 22 September and a week later Reickert announced the decision to the Product Planning Committee.

'Bobcat has got a name', he said. 'We'll call it Fiesta.'
Someone started to speak, but Reickert went on.
'Mr Ford chose the name himself. Are there any objections?'
They looked at each other and burst out laughing.
'Mr Ford will be pleased to hear that you agreed,' Reickert concluded. 'Just remember; it might have been called Adonis, Sonata, or Gato, if not Piccolo, Ischia or Bebe. All those names were on the original list!'

*

Bobcat is dead! Long live Fiesta!
Production was about to begin and soon Fiesta would cross the Atlantic. Fiesta is the first universal Ford car since the old Model T. Henry Ford I took the world by storm from his base at Dearborn. Henry Ford II, who was still in short pants when he accompanied his grandfather on his tours of inspection in Europe, chose a different launching pad for his own attempt at a one-car assault on world markets. The car boomerang is returning to America after a long European detour.

Henry Ford II has now been at the head of his empire for 30 years. He used to talk of retiring at 40. He is 59 and he has never grasped his sceptre as firmly as he does now. His son, Edsel II, 27, is patiently learning the job of being boss. He has already spent some time in the management of the design studios at Dearborn and with the business departments. He has quietly visited Europe. The succession is being prepared while the American market is in a state of turmoil. The energy crisis, the economic recession and new federal legislation have turned it upside down, but no one knows for sure whether it is a temporary change or a real revolution. It is a market which is becoming more European and more youth-orientated, so why not entrust it to a youthful 'European'? On 9 October 1975, deciding that his work in London was finished

Edsel Ford discovered the Ford Fiesta during a visit to Merkenich. Behind him is Jack Telnack, then vice president for design at Ford Europe.

and that he was ready for new exploits, this time on an American scale, Ford advised Bill Bourke that he had appointed him head of all the North American operations of the corporation, and offered him a seat on the Board. Bourke returned to Detroit after a long world tour by way of Canada, Australia and Europe and at 48, this promotion made him the third man in the whole Corporation after Henry Ford himself and Lee Iacocca. In London, John McDougall succeeded him as head of Ford-Europe, assisted by Harold Poling, a financial expert who learned of his promotion just as he was about to celebrate his fiftieth birthday.

So Bourke would not see Fiesta come off the production line at Saarlouis but he was to be in Dearborn to welcome it and perhaps to provide it with some compact, functional American cousins, inspired by the infants he cradled in Europe.

*

Press introduction of the Fiesta had been scheduled for 3 September, 1976, when sales were to start in Germany. Fiestas, however, were already rolling off the Saarlouis assembly line and being so rapidly distributed to Ford dealerships that press photographers had an easy task shooting the car from all angles. Leaks became so frequent that it appeared impossible to hold back official Fiesta news until September. Walter Hayes's public relations team decided to speed things up and introduced Fiesta to the press in June, with test drives starting in July.

The Fiesta launch turned out to be the automotive event of the year. Never before had a Ford car in Europe benefited from as wide a coverage, as enthusiastic a reception. The publicity was worth millions of dollars, and reporters successfully competed in playing with the Fiesta name in their headlines. Switzerland's *Blick* magazine hailed the car as a new 'Volks-Ford Fiesta', while many more insisted that Fiesta was to be 'no festival for the competition'. Appreciation ran from 'Mini-Ford' to 'Super-Ford', 'Super-Mini', and 'Maxi-Mini'.

Britain's *Car Magazine* ran a cover story under the heading 'Fiesta—bad news from Uncle Henry', only to explain that 'the new car could cause Leyland, Renault, Volkswagen, Fiat, and Peugeot no celebration at all!' A dozen magazines, including *Time*'s European edition, flashed the same obvious headline: 'What a Fiesta for Ford!' And Germany's *Wochenpresse* described the launch as 'a festival for the last one'.

Italy's *Gente Motori* summed up its first driving impressions with the simple statement: '800 billion lire well spent'. In England, *Motor's* technical editor Anthony Curtis referred to 'Ford's about-face Euro-car'. Some described Fiesta as 'mini-Ford, maxi-car', which Berlin's *Tagesblatt* summed up as 'small outside, large inside'. There were stories on 'a small car with great hopes', on 'the largest effort for the smallest car', on 'small car—big hit', and on 'small cars, huge competition'.

London's *Autocar* called Fiesta 'Ford's happy event', Germany's leading automotive magazine *Auto, Motor und Sport* published its first report under a two-word heading: 'Expensive techniques', the Paris Sunday paper *Journal du Dimanche* told its readers that Fiestas were 'fun and gay'. One of Belgium's leading auto writers Jacques Ickx—father of Formula 1 champion Jacky Ickx—mixed test impressions with fresh Olympic memories and compared Fiesta to Rumania's Olympic gymnastics star, calling Ford's new baby 'the Comaneci of the Automobile!'

Not everyone, of course, raved about the car. To some, it lacked originality. France's *L'Express* thought its design was a bit 'déjà vu', and many expressed fears that the Fiesta was late, if not too late. An *Autocar* editorial pointed out that 'market research is a fickle animal, and it has led manufacturers astray in the past. In America during the 1973 fuel crisis Detroit was convinced that everyone wanted small cars, production lines were torn up and Detroit's idea of a small car was soon cascading into the dealerships. Now there is evidence that they moved too soon, and that while the American public may well have told the researchers that they wanted small economical cars at the height of the publicity about the lack of petrol and the patriotic need to conserve, what they *really* wanted was still large, comfortable, heavy, chromed status symbols'.

Ford, to tell the truth, had not been misled by its own market researchers, as demonstrated by Henry Ford's decision *not* to manufacture the car in the U.S., but only import it in reasonable quantity until until the market would eventually give a different answer. At the same time, Europe started demonstrating that local Ford analysts had been right also: Fiesta was neither too small nor too late, even though a sharp upswing in the economy again seemed to drive the public away from mini-cars to larger size vehicles.

Ford dealers introduced Fiesta in Germany and Northern Europe (with the exception of Great Britain where sales were to start only 2 February, 1977) on 3 September, 1976, in Italy on 4 September, and in France on 9 September. With the exception of press reports, not a cent had been spent on advertising at that point. Firm advance orders had been registered nonetheless for 33,000 cars—a 'pre-sell' total of over $100 million. One month later, advance orders were up to 45,000 units, and 20,000 Fiestas were already in the hands of their new and often proud owners. Germany's *Bild am Sonntag* reported on the impressions of the first Fiesta buyer of them all, a 35-year-old lawyer in Cologne, Hellmuth Völlings. 'What a car,' Völlings told reporters. 'It sure is a feast!' Völling had previously owned a VW bug, a Ford 20 MTS, and an Audi 100 GLS. 'Instead of having one large car,' he said, 'my wife and I decided to buy two Fiestas. We like the Fiesta because it is roomy, comfortable, fast enough, and economical. We also like the fact that so many traditional options are standard on this one.'

Bernd Völlings, 8, added this comment to his father's: 'What I like is the loudspeakers in the back. I can hear the music even when Dad drives fast!'

*

Of course, market analysts could not satisfy themselves with interviews like that one. Even before Fiesta was being sold officially, a group of researchers started camping in Ford dealerships in Germany, France, and Italy in mid-August to

244

produce a series of weekly marketing reports, first on 'presell buyers' and later on 'Fiesta shoppers and buyers'.

The first of these reports, which sales vice-president Gordon MacKenzie passed on to his colleagues on 23 August, confirmed most of the findings and hopes expressed by researchers two and three years earlier. Comments by R.P. Smith, head of marketing research, were highly encouraging. Findings were based on 250 interviews of buyers at 30 main dealerships in Germany, France, and Italy.

'In all three markets,' Smith noted, 'Fiesta appears to be much more incremental to Ford than other B-cars to their manufacturers. Over the three markets as a whole, only 13 per cent of Fiesta buyers claim they would have bought some other Ford if Fiesta had not existed. Compare this implied low level of substitution with that achieved by Fiat 127 in Italy, VW Polo in Germany, and Renault 5 in France—51 per cent, 47 per cent, and 23 per cent of whose buyers respectively say they would have bought some other same-make car if their present model had not existed.'

It was obvious from the start that Fiesta sales would to a very large extent be conquest sales, with little effect on Escort distribution. The survey clearly demonstrated that three Fiesta buyers in every five had never owned a Ford before at any time. The report further showed sharp differences between Escort and Fiesta buyers:

'Compared with Escort, nearly twice as many Fiesta sales are to multi-car families (42 per cent versus 23 per cent), nearly three times as many are to first-time or add-on buyers (19 per cent versus 7 per cent), and nearly four times as many are to women buyers (27 per cent versus 7 per cent). The Fiesta buyer also tends to be younger (nearly three in five are under 35 as against one in two), with a smaller family, and more often single.'

It was also reported that half of the pre-sold cars were in the 'L' version and one-quarter were base models. 'S' series sales were double those of the Ghia luxury version (17 per cent versus 8 per cent). Finally, two-thirds of sales at that early stage were with the smaller 957 cc engine.

Coming in at the rate of one a week, further 'capsule reports' perfectly confirmed earlier findings. The last of these reports, based on nearly 1,000 interviews of shoppers and buyers in three countries, was released on 1 October, less than one week before Fiesta's official world debut at the Paris Auto Show. Of the three markets under review, Italy was clearly the most receptive: 86 per cent of all Italian showroom visitors found the car 'excellent' or 'very good' and predicted it would sell 'very well', as against 79 per cent in France and only 69 per cent in Germany, where 30 per cent of the visitors found that it was 'a good car, but not that much better than most others'.

This was confirmed by the fact that 32 per cent of Fiesta shoppers in Italy, against 24 per cent in France and 19 per cent in Germany placed an immediate order or decided to 'definitely buy', which was better on average than similar results achieved at the time of launch by the latest Escort and Taunus models.

When asked what they liked most about Fiesta, prospects named styling and appearance as the main assets, followed by interior roominess, compact size, variable luggage capacity, interior appearance, technical design, and comfort. A few of the Italians criticized luggage capacity, Frenchmen were unhappy with seats and some aspects of finish and appointment, and Germans said they had been hoping for a more favorable price tag.

Despite these scattered negative remarks, the survey showed an exceptionally high degree of approval. When asked to compare Fiesta with its main competitor in each market—VW Polo in Germany, Renault 5 in France, and Fiat 127 in Italy—showroom visitors considered that the newcomer was a 'better car' in the proportion of 90 per cent in Germany, 89 per cent in Italy, and 85 per cent in France. The high level of conquest sales was confirmed: no more than 12 per cent of Fiesta buyers in all three markets (and only 8 per cent in Italy) claimed that they would have bought some other Ford if Fiestas had not existed. Three in every five Fiesta buyers never owned a Ford at any time. 63 per cent ordered the 957 cc engine, 37 per cent the larger one. The base model accounted for 24 per cent of all sales, the 'L' for 47 per cent, the 'S' for 17 per cent, and the Ghia version for 12 per cent.

Seventy-nine per cent of sales were replacements for existing cars, mostly Fiats (18 per cent), VW-Audis (9 per cent), Renaults (9 per cent), Citroens (5 per cent), Chrysler Simcas (4 per cent), and Leyland Minis (3 per cent)—which clearly showed who was going to lose most as a consequence of Fiesta's launch.

A by-product of the survey was of some interest to Ford's marketing staff: the report showed that salesmen in France and in Italy did a much better job than their counterparts in Germany. Only 68 per cent of German dealers bothered to speak to visitors, against 84 per cent in Italy and 83 per cent in France; while 82 per cent of Italian salesmen quoted a price, only 43 per cent did in Germany. Four out of five visitors in the Latin countries had the privilege of having the car door opened for them, against one German in two. A salesman development programme is now under way in Germany...

*

Henry Ford and Lee Iacocca got the good news in London on 18 October, on their way to Spain where they were to see some of the first Spanish Fiestas roll off the assembly line one week later. King Juan Carlos joined them in Almusafes on 25 October, together with scores of government officials.

'We are here,' Henry Ford said, 'because we have confidence in the future of Spain, the vitality of its economy, and the quality of its workers. We are here because the Spanish government was confident that we knew what we were doing and would keep our commitments. And we are here because we have faith in the continuing growth of a European economy and a Europe-wide motor vehicle market in which Spain will play an integral and increasingly important rôle. In the process, I believe we will also contribute to the realization of a larger vision— a vision of Western Europe as a place where each nation preserves its national identity but where the peace and prosperity of all nations is assured by their growing economic cooperation and interdependence.'

In that respect, Ford had obviously set an example with Fiesta, the first truly 'multinational car'.

A huge promotion and advertising programme was being conducted all over Europe describing Fiesta as *la concurrente* (the competitor) in France, *una forte rivale* (a strong rival) in Italy, and *the new format car* in Germany. Press statements were issued at regular intervals to underline the production and sales progress of the new car. It was announced in mid-October that 50,000 cars had already been assembled at Saarlouis. Italy claimed 10,000 sales one month after introduction, and France made it public by the end of November that 20,000 orders had already been registered. By 1 December, Bordeaux had produced its 100,000th gear box and Almusafes its 100,000th engine. By the end of the year, Saarlouis in turn would have put out 100,000 cars as the Spanish and British assembly plants were joining in the huge continental carrousel.

The best news, however, was coming from Spain at this time. After a thorough inspection of Fiestas assembled in Almusafes, Ford of Europe quality engineers reported to headquarters:

'The level of workmanship at Almusafes and the basic assembly quality is just as good in Spain, from the start, as it is in our German plant at Saarlouis.'

Some even claimed that Spanish Fiestas were better. Considering that Saarlouis had the best quality record in Europe until then, and that both the Almusafes factory and men were brand new, this was possibly the greatest achievement of the whole programme.

*

As a welcome promotional support and as a possible preview of future attractions, Ghia lost no time producing two show cars derived from Ford's latest baby. The Corrida and the Prima were displayed at the Turin Auto Show, right under Fiat's nose, at the beginning of November.

The Corrida was based on the Fiesta 1117 cc S mechanicals and illustrated a few original ideas: gull wing type side doors with a second hinge along the center line just below the windows, the lower part of the door folding inwards when open; a sort of drawer type rear trunk, to be pulled out for loading, along with a top-hinged rear window opening upwards. The front came with an elongated nose contributing to the futuristic appearance of this Corrida. As for the Prima, it was a 4-in-1 construction, basically a pick-up body on which could be attached any of four rear end body styles—flat-decked pick-up, two-seater coupé with separate boot, 2 + 2 fastback, or four-seater station wagon.

Engineers kept just as busy as designers. They were already developing a 1.3 litre version of the car, and specialist teams were hard at work giving the finishing touches to several sports versions of Fiesta, including a 240 hp model for Rally Cross competition.

The main effort, however, went into 'federalizing' Fiesta for the U.S. market. Several product feasibility studies had been undertaken, including import of a federalized version of the European Fiesta in a K.D. or 'knocked down' form to be assembled in the U.S. Once the Board decided not to assemble the car in America at first but to import it as a finished product from Europe, a special team had to be set up urgently to work on adapting the car to the U.S. market. Dick Edwards, who had played a major part in designing Fiesta for Europe, was transfered to Detroit in charge of the programme. After many others, he discovered the joys and hardships of commuting constantly between Dunton, Cologne, and Dearborn before the final U.S. version was developed. The basic ground rules set for the vehicle were to accommodate all federal requirements but to change the European Fiestas as little as possible. Even with this mandate, however, the U.S. version ended up having 559 unique parts, which shows how large an effort such an adaptation implied.

The first decision, of course, was to fit the car with the 1600 cc Kent engine, modified to accept the transverse axle and to abide by U.S. emission rules.

Another fundamental choice was the selection of a carburetor for the 1600 cc engine. Neither the Belfast Ford carburetor utilized on the European Fiesta nor the U.S. Holly 5200 used on the 2300 cc Pinto engine were applicable. A decision was made to utilize the Italian-made Weber Datra unit. However, even the Datra unit required extensive redesign to accommodate U.S. emission requirements. So Ford U.S. became involved in the design, development, and testing of a carburetor which originated in Italy for installation in Germany on all cars to be sold in the U.S.—another example of the complexity of worldwide engineering and the communications challenge facing Ford engineers in the U.S. and Europe.

As other component source decisions were made, the world-wide purchasing market was again considered. Among those suppliers selected were Ford Motor Company's U.S.-based Glass Division, supplying windshields, side and rear glass; and the Electrical and Electronics Division providing turn signals, lamp assemblies, alternators, and regulators. In addition, 15 other U.S.-based outside suppliers were selected to provide parts utilized in the assembly of the U.S. Fiesta.

While the U.S. Fiesta product programme was launched as a minimum change effort, except for federally mandated standards, one important U.S. option, air conditioning, was added. As the car had been originally designed with no provision for air conditioning, the task was assigned to Dearborn engineers to provide package space for the air conditioning compressor and other hardware in the engine compartment.

U.S. engineers made a number of package studies which were coordinated with their counterparts in Ford of Europe. Because air conditioning was a late entry into the programme, Ford of Europe was forced to restart a number of durability and design tests which were already under way or even completed.

Forrest Poling, when taking over from Dick Edwards as overall coordinator of the U.S. Fiesta, had to get involved in a number of other modifications. One such instance took place because the battery used in the European Fiesta was not readily available in the U.S. In order to avoid a replacement part availability problem, a different battery had to be selected. The new U.S. battery ended up larger than its European counterpart, so the battery tray had to be redesigned and then the revised battery and tray had to be retested to assure that they, along with the newly developed air conditioning unit, would all pass the necessary crash tests.

Jim Chandler, in charge of the engine and emissions development for the U.S. Fiesta, was faced with a number of unique problems. Experience with a 1600 cc engine in a vehicle weighing less than 2,000 pounds was virtually non-existent, particularly in terms of meeting federal emissions requirements. With no Fiesta prototype vehicles available, the early emissions test work was done in the U.S. using Ford Escort vehicles with 1600 cc engines. Later on hand-assembled prototype Fiesta 1600 cc engines were used in Fiats 'cobbled' to resemble Fiestas.

When the U.S. Fiesta programme was approved the plan called for design work, testing, and Environmental Protection Agency certification to be completed in time for Saarlouis to start production on 31 January 1977. Because of the long transit time, public introduction in the U.S. was originally set for mid-April, 1977. This, however, was too aggressive a timetable. It provided almost no turn-around time. As the programme developed, component modifications requiring design changes and retesting led to a delay in the target date. Vehicle assembly was therefore rescheduled to begin in late March, 1977.

As the product development effort progressed, Ford Division began developing the marketing plan for the car. Much had happened in the market since approval of the U.S. Fiesta programme. The energy crisis had subsided and the foreign car—small car share of total U.S. car sales had decreased from the record levels of 1974-1975. Short term objectives had to be redefined. Shortly afterward, Jon Deimel was appointed Fiesta sales manager, with the responsibility of coordinating the whole launch effort.

Deimel started developing a franchising plan. When Ford Division began importing the Courier truck from Japan, dealers were franchised both selectively and regionally. Because of Fiesta's higher sales volume forecast and in view of the long-term nationwide growth in the small car market, it was decided to offer the Fiesta franchise to all Ford dealers at one time.

Once the decision was made as to who was to sell Fiestas, it had to be determined how the car would be allocated to dealers, both at the time of launch and on an ongoing basis. Because of the long-lead time involved in importing the Fiesta (5 months from initial production schedule to arrival at dealerships), the first several months of Fiesta production had to be ordered—with complete specifications for each car—well before the first unit was to be sold. Therefore, the launch plan had to define the number of units that each dealer should receive and the complete specifications for each car. With four trim levels, seven exterior colors, and seventeen options, the Fiesta was a very complex vehicle. Putting the right car in dealer hands to assure a successful launch was a major challenge.

More clinics were set up and more research was conducted to finally develop a marketing plan for Fiesta, with one major communications objective: precisely define the target audience for the new car, and also clearly assess Fiesta's major strengths in the minds of this audience.

The corporation, from top to bottom, took part in this new drive, promoting Fiesta long before it reached U.S. shores. 'We invested close to one billion dollars in Fiesta,' Henry Ford announced publicly. 'We will invest 15 billion dollars over the next ten years to open a new era for the automobile.'

'Watch out for Fiesta,' Lee Iacocca told the press. 'We know the Volkswagen Rabbit is a good car. So is Fiesta. And Fiesta will be cheaper than the Rabbit.'

'The development of small cars like Fiesta with potential for world development is one of the most exciting and significant events in the history of the motor vehicle,' Bill Bourke told the annual meeting of the General Motors Institute Alumni Association. 'The advantages of a universal car are enormous. Obviously, there would be huge cost savings. No longer would we have to engineer, style, or market a flock of totally different cars to meet the special tastes and needs of different countries. There would also be highly significant advantages in production and marketing. Our transnational planning would make the greatest possible use of local capabilities and situations—like making transmissions in one country, drive-trains in another, engines in a third, and putting them all together in several places—as we are doing with the Fiesta in Europe.'

The Fiesta was shown not only as a revolution within Ford, but possibly as the first car in a new era of automobile history.

*

After a quarter of a century of waiting and hoping, the Bobcat-Fiesta programme has been carried out in just about four years, a record time considering the immense new problems involved. Similar projects had been rejected on several occasions. Probably they were not sufficiently well thought out. But above all, their chances of success were slender at a time when competing cars were more often than not being sold at a loss or at cost price. A reader unfamiliar with the subject may be irritated at the references to profits, margins and returns on capital which crop up so often in this story. Nevertheless they are part of the rules of the game. Ford are not subsidised or supported by anyone; they can count on no one but their thousands of shareholders, who in their turn depend on Ford. There are some individuals and institutions with large blocks of shares, but the majority are small stockholders, many of them Ford employees; and not just senior staff either, but technicians, clerks and factory workers.

Henry Ford often says: 'I am responsible to them just as I am responsible to our employees and to the public in general.'

This is why Fiesta was held back for so long. One can indulge personal preferences for one kind of car or another, one may dream of building Rolls-Royces or Ferraris, but when one's name is Ford, when one has 450,000 employees on five continents, and 350,000 shareholders scattered around the world, there is one right that is denied, and that is the right to gamble.

Fiesta was thought out, conceived and developed within the framework of public demand and the potential of an existing company. It evolved through a continuous coming and going between Europe and America to become one of the most

Ford Europe top brass during the last check of the final prototype at Merkenich.
From left to right: Lew Veraldi (Vice President — Product Development), Uwe
Bahnsen (Vice President — Design), John McDougall (Chairman), Red Poling
(President), Gordon MacKenzie (Vice President — Sales) and Erik Reickert (Vice
President — Product Planning).

advanced projects in the history of the modern motor industry. Everything was new this time: the car, the techniques, the factories, the people. Bobcat would have disappeared without trace if Eagle had not first taken wing. Enormous resources were mobilised on an inter-continental scale. New methods, new systems, new techniques were brought into play. No programme was ever controlled so meticulously or carried through with such strict discipline. This was the only way that this immense and hazardous venture could be brought to a successful conclusion.

And it was hazardous, for all the careful planning, as anything so vast, so ambitious and so costly must be. There is no country in Europe that has not contributed in some way to the accomplishment of this programme and there will be very few which do not benefit from it. When it is all added up, Ford are backing a little 1500 lb. car, less than twelve feet long, with over a billion dollars.

Europe will never see another project on this scale. The traditional markets are becoming saturated; the high price of energy improverishes the West; cars are under attack in the countries which are already crammed with them. If there is ever another programme comparable with Bobcat, it might well be in a different part of the world, in a different environment. Latin America has not had its last word, Asia and Africa have barely had their first. For the industrialised countries, Bobcat marks the end of an era and the beginning of a new one. For this reason the preceding pages may perhaps have some small historical interest.

The story of its birth ends here, just as Ford's Fiesta is invading Europe, America, and the world. The real challenge implicit in the whole Bobcat project is only beginning.

Saint Canadet, January 1977.

Edouard Seidler in conversation with Henry Ford II.

Edouard Seidler had the rare privilege of being intimately associated with the whole Fiesta project. A journalist and writer, he is one of the best informed observers of the automotive world. Now 45, he is the editorial director of *L'Equipe*, the largest sports and automotive daily paper in the world. His writings appear in numerous trade papers throughout the world. He is the author of several books on the automobile, including *World Champion* (an account of Jackie Stewart's and Matra's climb to fame), *The great voices of the automobile* (a series of interviews with leaders of the industry) and *The Romance of Renault*. A graduate of the School of Political Science in Paris, and a holder of a Master's degree in Business Administration of the University of California at Los Angeles, Edouard Seidler received several awards in recognition of his journalistic and literary achievements in favour of the automobile, including the Prix Pierre About (1966), the Harold Pemberton Trophy of the Guild of Motoring Writers (1971), and the Prix de Liedekerque-Beaufort of the Automobile Club de France (1974).

This book was created and produced by Edita S.A.
Lausanne - Switzerland